THE DAMNDEST FINEST RUINS

The Damndest Finest

Ruins MONICA SUTHERLAND

Coward-McCann, Inc. NEW YORK

*Photographic Illustrations will be found
following page 112.*

INTRODUCTORY NOTE

San Francisco has long been one of the most writ-ten-about of American cities. Indeed, books dealing with one phase or another of its history have become so numerous that it would, one might think, be all but impossible to hit on a subject that hasn't already been well-worn by earlier writers. Yet, such is the hold the place has on the affections of people all over the globe, and such is the variety and color of its back-ground, that not only do new San Francisco titles appear on publishers' lists most seasons but each con-tinues to find its audience of enthusiastic readers.

While this little volume adds yet another to the

5

list of San Francisco books, it has a number of points that set it apart. For one thing, it treats of but a single episode—though a highly important one—in the town's history and, for another, it is told from the viewpoint, not of the sober (and sometimes heavy-handed) historical writer, but of an observant, ingenuous and thoroughly enamored visitor from England.

Monica Sutherland's love affair with the City by the Bay had its beginning during a stay there in 1957. Oddly enough, her interest was first stirred, not by the Gold Rush or some other chapter of the city's romantic beginnings, but by a comparatively recent event; namely, the earthquake and fire of 1906. A survivor herself of the 1939–1945 London bombings, Miss Sutherland had some knowledge of city dwellers in the midst of catastrophe. Yet it is clear also that, like many another visitor, she was intrigued—and puzzled —at the spectacle of three-quarters of a million people living practically on top of two major earthquake faults, seemingly indifferent to the fact that they might at any moment be caught in an upheaval and shaken until their teeth rattled.

No doubt responding to the redoubtable qualities of these western city dwellers of a half century earlier, the author began her inquiry into the behavior of those who had undergone just such an experience. In any event hers was a rewarding quest, for her researches brought to light as engaging a mass of fact and fancy, of solid history and wild imaginings, as one is likely to encounter in months of reading. It is, moreover, easy to understand why that was so. For the author got a great deal of her material at first hand from residents who themselves had lived through the ordeal—and if there's one thing above all others that old-time San Franciscans love to do, it's to talk about—and embroider on—their experiences during what they always refer to as "the fire."

The story that results is a spirited and, in many respects, an inspiring one. For from it we learn how, on the morning of April 18, 1906, the residents were jolted from their beds by one of the severest quakes the country has ever known; of how, during the next three days—their fire-fighting equipment made useless by lack of water—they watched the flames sweep through the heart of their city; and finally how, while the ashes were yet warm, they gamely set about plans for rebuilding on a larger, far more impressive scale.

It is a story of excitement, of adventure, and of courage; one that well deserves to be remembered. And when, as in the present instance, it is pictured from the viewpoint of an admiring—and admirable— visitor from across the sea, this lends a certain tang and piquancy to the telling that its readers will find highly agreeable.

—OSCAR LEWIS

7

FOREWORD

WHEN I traveled to San Francisco in the early summer of 1957 I had no idea at all of what the place would look like. I had spent some time in the eastern part of the continent, and everyone I met, on hearing that I hoped to stay for some weeks in San Francisco, said at once, "How lucky you are; you'll love it, it's so beautiful." But so many Americans to whom I spoke had never been there. They were strongly aware of the magnetic attraction of the place, but though they would dearly love to make the journey it was, after all, a long way off. Those who knew the city—some of them intimately— all said much the same

9

thing, but not a single soul ever described it to me even in the simplest terms.

As for myself, born and bred in England, San Francisco from my earliest days at school had been and remained a famous, exotic place with a brightly colored history behind it, six thousand miles from my home. I had never considered its physical aspect; I knew that it was beautiful, but the beauty of cities for me was that of Vienna or Budapest—a thoroughly European conception, the glory of which had never been seriously challenged by any place I knew in the eastern part of the American continent. On the vast map of the United States it appeared as a not particularly impressive finger of land in relation to the great coastline of the Pacific Ocean.

So it was that I came fresh and unaware to one of the greatest experiences of my life. The wonder of San Francisco conquered me; I fell in love and knew that the love would last for my lifetime. Because of my love of the city, and because I felt bound to try to share some of it not only with my own countrymen but also with those Americans who had never been to San Francisco, I have attempted to give some sort of a picture of the city's unique natural beauty, the beauty, that is, not only of the city itself—and that is impressive enough—but of its situation, the like of which can surely not be found anywhere else.

And in considering San Francisco, ancient and modern, one is bound to consider the Disaster of 1906.

Many people have asked me why I, who lived through the bombing and saw the terrible effects of the 1939–45 war in Europe, should be interested in the details of an earthquake and fire which lasted only for five days and caused surprisingly few casualties. "Surely," they say, "after what you have seen and experienced in Europe the San Francisco Disaster must seem like a very old potato." But the two things have little connection in my mind, and, if they had, I could find many reasons for my interest in the San Francisco affair. For example, the world then had not been subjected to the man-made horrors of global warfare which it has known since. The reaction of ordinary people to conditions of appalling trial and anxiety of that kind had not been tested. And it is interesting to find that in their time of danger the people of the city of the Far West showed the very same qualities of courage, patience, and humor that characterized Londoners when they were ruthlessly attacked from the air, night after night, in the autumn of 1940; homes were wrecked, everything seemed lost, yet life had to go on notwithstanding. Both cities were confronted with a dreadful and hitherto unknown emergency; both at once rose to the occasion with splendid spirit and an obstinate refusal to be conquered by any ordeal, however great, that they might be called on to suffer. Americans, English, and many other European nations reacted in precisely the same way in the face of extreme danger and crippling loss.

But in her time of severe trial England was at war; the civilian population, aware that for the first time they too were in the "firing line," were in a sense prepared for devastation and death in the streets of their cities. The horribly awe-inspiring quality of the San Francisco affair was that it was a "natural" disaster. The terror that assaulted the inhabitants came from below, from the very earth on which the city's phenomenal prosperity had been built and on which it depended for its existence. And it tormented a population that was still many years away from experience of the wholesale ruin that can be caused by the hatred of man for men. One common denominator exists: the shining courage of ordinary people confronted by extraordinary perils. That, if nothing else, should give hope for the future of the world, whatever its destiny may ultimately prove to be.

In thinking of what I have written and of my stay in San Francisco I feel deeply grateful to all those kind people who invited me to their homes, wrote to me, or telephoned me, and have allowed me to publish their personal stories of the Disaster. They did not know me, I was a "foreigner," yet all made me welcome and did their best to help me. I should also like to thank Mr. James de T. Abajian, of the California Historical Society, and Miss Corter, of the San Francisco Public Library, for constant help and advice. Nor must I forget Mr. Walter Pilkington, who put the resources of the library at Hamilton College, Clinton, New York, at my disposal and gave me so much encouragement. Of the celebrated Bohemian Club in San Francisco I can speak only from hearsay since no woman is allowed to cross its portals. But the Secretary, Mr. Herzog, was extremely kind to my husband, Humphrey Sutherland, who went there for me, and supplied him with a bibliography for my use. Mr. Bayard Schieffelin and Mr. Archibald de Weese of the New York Public Library, and Mr. Fred Adams, Jr., of the Pierpont Morgan Library, were very kind in helping me on various points.

Finally I should like to thank George and Barbara Blackwell who not only gave me many introductions, but also did me the great practical kindness of lending me a car. Without their help my work would have been much more difficult and many happy interviews impossible.

My grateful thanks are due for permission to quote the poem by Mr. Lawrence W. Harris in Chapter Nine.

PROLOGUE

AN ordinary map of California such as is given away at American gas stations is the first thing that begins to convey the beguiling, insidious charm of San Francisco. For those to whom it has hitherto been only an inconspicuous little finger on the west side of America's great coastline, the geographical position of the city, enlarged against the background of the state, suddenly begins to assert itself. For the natural shape of the place is as astonishing as that of any other place in the world.

From Monterey Bay the continent narrows down, preparing itself, as it were, for the geographical revelation to come. And as the eye of the traveler scans the printed scene on his map he rapidly becomes aware of a great index finger pointing northward to the rest of the continent, but itself ending in the sea. Maps paint the sea blue, as is only proper, and the index finger is seen to be surrounded not by other fingers of a giant hand, but by the blue of sea, fashioned into beautifully rounded shapes, framing the narrow neck of land on the tip of which, on the very tip, lies San Francisco. A stranger looking for the Queen of the West naturally expects a city set upon a long Pacific coastline. What he is unprepared for is the enormous Bay of San Francisco combined with the almost absurdly narrow ocean entrance of the Golden Gate itself —fifty miles of Bay with a Gate one mile wide. The depth of that blue water, deep enough for the very largest ships, was long ago discovered and made use of. But on a map it has a quality of unreality, particularly when it is compared with the spacious, rounded shapes of the bays to which it is the only approach and without which they would lose their entire significance. And up into the middle of the whole fantastically shaped complex points the finger of the city of San Francisco, the fabulous town daringly built by the gold men on a site surrounded on three sides by the sea. It is only when the eye lights on the two rearing shapes, the Golden Gate Bridge, still imaginatively orange-painted, and the Bay Bridge in the more conventional silver, that the traveler realizes that the city is a busy heart which would cease to beat if it had not got those great arteries to join it all ways to the mainland, both giving and receiving life.

A roadside map may be the starting point of enchantment but, in case the exploring traveler is not yet fully satisfied about the beauty of the city of which he has heard so much, a yet stronger spell may be laid on the imagination before he actually enters the place itself. From the top of Mount Tamalpais, the mountain where the Indian Princess lies forever, the features of her face outlined against the sky, her long hair flowing down to the sea, a physical view more potent than any printed map delights and charms the senses. From that height—and it is not very high by mountain standards—the whole of San Francisco and its pattern of bays lies spread out in a spectacular colored design. The surrounding satellite towns, separated from their great mother by sea, yet still by virtue of the bridges in close relationship to her, lie flat upon the sides of the land. The steepness is ironed out by distance, and dramatic shapes made by land and sea in happy conjunction are strongly emphasized by the thousands upon thousands of houses built there during the last fifty years.

In the distance the city of San Francisco, the giant index finger, lies small, glittering, and pointed, like some intricately worked jewel along the tip of the Peninsula. There are some trees in the city—oleanders and other charming things covered with flowers at the proper season—but they are not to be seen from that distance. The place is like a porcelain ornament, the product of some seventeenth-century French factory, fragile, beautiful, and lovingly hand-worked on different levels to give light and shade. The age-old factory which, as it seems to an imagination stimulated by the idea of a china set-piece, produced the marvel, had craftsmen who possessed the secrets of the centuries and who knew how to use them for the utter delight of mankind. For scale they threw in Telegraph Hill with its fantastic Coit Tower, and contentedly made of the rest the most intricate and most beautiful of designs.

The sun and the wonderful clarity of the air show the marvel to perfection. Yet, beyond the narrow opening of the Golden Gate waits the low-lying bank of cloud—or fog as San Franciscans call it—present even on the hottest day. The waterfall of mist tumbles down over the hills and stretches out in long veils toward the enchanted city. At any time, without any notice, it may decide to cover the whole picture, so that even the nightly fascination of myriads of lights is completely invisible. The air, hot maybe with midday sun, is cooled and washed, and the clean white city emerges clothed in beauty for another day.

Yet, after all, San Francisco is a modern city built for trade a bare hundred years ago and rebaptized after the great Disaster of 1906. What is it like at close quarters today? At its heart it is, like other American cities, rectangular; but somehow it does not seem so.

This is partly because the plan is not complete, but mainly because of the falling terraces of its hills, cutting across the street plans. It is a city of wide streets except downtown, where narrow streets seem narrower because of a modest sprinkling of not very tall skyscrapers.

Elsewhere street width is accentuated by a general lowness of building height, which admits the full clear light of a clean, cloud-washed sky. But spaciousness and lightness never mean monotony in San Francisco. The architecture is superbly varied, going back from the latest window-pierced cubes through Edwardian stone-and-brick splendor (all columns and heavy moldings and turrets) to the simpler, lighter forms of wooden houses perpetuating the nineteenth-century tradition. Added to these styles is the tinge of Spanish elegance in many a small private house, the monstrous decorum of "official" classical in public buildings, and the blue water of the harbor as the farthest setting of any hilltop view of the city.

The place is quite extraordinarily steep. It has been said that most of the best things in San Francisco are free but that a strong pair of legs is needed to climb the hills. Of course, there are always the cable cars clanging up and down the steepest of them—the same form of transportation that was used in the days of the Disaster. San Franciscans are fond of the cable cars and allow themselves the luxury of that particular sentimentality. The cables lie beneath the road; there are driver and conductor—and a special brake behind in case of any

19

unforeseen danger on one of the steepest hills. Passengers sit facing outward—as on an Irish jaunting car—and everyone enjoys the ride, especially the children. The clanging bell, the warning of an approaching car, is a feature and once a year a contest is held for the "fanciest ring."

Terrace after terrace falls steeply to a bright, busy, and varied waterfront, where miles of shipping piers are followed by another mile of seafood shops fronted by great cauldrons of boiling crabs, delicious to eat and picturesque to see. And the whole busy, elegant, active city gives a charming impression of being pink and white all over; dirt and grime simply have no place in the color plan of the Queen of the West. The beautiful scene, decked everywhere with flowers, giant butterflies, and birds with bright plumage, has a Mediterranean quality which is belied only by the icy cold of the brilliant blue Pacific Ocean. San Francisco, once seen, retains a magnetic influence on the memory, for it is one of the wonders of the world.

ONE

FRANCIS DRAKE, called by his friends a great sailor and by his enemies a detestable pirate, narrowly missed discovering the Golden Gate entrance to the Bay of San Francisco. Had he found it he would no doubt have christened the peninsula New Albion, and later on America might have had to fight a war of independence against Britain on her western as well as her eastern seaboard.

In December 1577 he sailed from England in an attempt to voyage right around the world. He had the blessing of Queen Elizabeth I (who also paid for the expedition) and he was in company with five

21

other small vessels and one hundred and sixty-six men.

Drake was a master of success, and that expedition was no exception to the rest of his career. He sailed up the western coast of America by way of Chile and Peru, victoriously attacking and plundering every Spanish ship he met with on the way. By the time he reached northern California three of the other ships had been separated from him and had returned to England. But, undismayed, Drake sailed on, up the long, strange coast washed by the fierce tides of the unknown Pacific Ocean.

It was a vast expanse of sea to be chartered by such small sailing vessels, and though the expedition must have passed very near to the Golden Gate they never saw it. But it was necessary to land somewhere. The ships, laden down with the gold and silver of Peru, had to be overhauled before they could safely make the long voyage back to England, and anchor was finally dropped in a sandy cove in Marin County (now called Drake's Bay) a few miles north of the San Francisco Peninsula. There, as was his custom, Drake erected a tablet recording his landing, and called the place New Albion in honor of England.

Although he could not know it, Drake had dropped anchor in earthquake country. He and his men hardly   ved long enough to be alarmed by the strange   nomenon of a shock, but his chosen beach was well within the earthquake belt, mapped out hundreds of years later, which runs from the north to the south of America on the western seaboard. Nor could he know, when he sailed up the Thames in September 1580 to meet his queen (who, with the happy personal touch for which she was famous, went down to Deptford and knighted him on board the ship in which he had made his historic voyage), that the famous city of the West, the site of which he had so nearly discovered, would be called after the saint whose Christian name he bore. Two Franciscan friars eventually founded the city for Spain, and the English mariner is commemorated only in the name of a modern hotel.

After their fortunate escape from the English, the Californian Indians of the interior remained undisturbed for a long time. Their history is still mysterious, and the marks of their fires on the giant redwood trees in Muir Woods seem to strike a truer chord in the imagination than any of their legendary doings on contemporary television. What does, however, seem certain is that though the Spanish, when they arrived, did penetrate from time to time into Indian territory, it was a long time before they attempted any kind of settlement there. They took and held the coastal strip with little more than a hundred men and did not at first trouble themselves with the country that lay behind.

Don Gaspar de Portola, Governor of Lower California, was the first to arrive. He had left San Diego on an overland expedition in search of Monterey and, apparently by chance, discovered the San Francisco Peninsula. He reported his find on returning home, but did not leave anyone to occupy the desolate spot. Six years later, in 1775, Don Manuel Ayala sailed through the Golden Gate in the *San Carlos*, a packet of the Spanish navy and the first ship to pass through that famous water gate from the Pacific. The following year a land expedition commanded by Don Juan Bautista Anza finally arrived on the Peninsula with the determination to establish a Spanish colony.

On his expedition from San Diego in 1769 De Portola had taken his Franciscan confessor with him, and when Ayala arrived he had in his company two Franciscan friars named Cambon and Palon. Wherever they went the Spaniards concerned themselves to establish two main things: the Spanish religion and the Spanish way of life, including its amusements as well as its military installations. It followed, therefore, that while Colonel Ayala founded the Presidio to the north of the Peninsula the friars occupied themselves with the creation of the Mission Dolores, famous throughout the history of San Francisco, and now perhaps the oldest building in the city.

The Spaniards adopted a deliberate policy toward the Indians. They envisaged the retention of the na-

tives as the basis of the population and they employed them—by force, if need be—in useful pursuits.
More than that, Spain even encouraged racial
mixture, and miscegenation apparently did not hold
the terrors for them that it did for the Anglo-Ameri-
cans who followed them in California. Ibero-Ameri-
cans utilized the natives and incorporated them in
their economic structure, whereas Anglo-Ameri-
cans rigidly excluded them from the social order;
their system had no place for them and no bond
could be found which could mitigate the indifference
and contempt with which they were regarded. When
the Missions were eventually secularized more than
30,000 Indians, partly civilized and accustomed to be
cared for by the Fathers, were left unprotected and
were despoiled and exploited as never before.

In those early days San Francisco was named
Yerba Buena—literally the "good herb," which may
well have been the common, fragrant, and health-
giving mint that flourishes everywhere there today.
Life went on peacefully and quietly in the new colony, and the settlers were happy and contented in the
sunny freshness of the Peninsula. The missionaries
busied themselves with making wine and brandy, as
well as cultivating the soil, and their products, together with such things as tallow and hides, were
exchanged for necessary goods brought into the Bay
by Spanish ships from the south. There were fiestas,
cockfights, and rodeos, and every advantage was

25

taken of the wonderfully temperate climate to promote outdoor entertainment.

Spanish-style architecture—still widely seen today —sprang up everywhere. Adobe walls with broad, stucco-covered, undecorated wall faces; arcaded corridors or *portales,* low-pitched red-tiled roofs with wide projecting eaves—all these things became typical of building in San Francisco, though as yet the population was very small. To add to the charming appearance of the happy village, houses were often built around a patio with a garden and fountain at the center, the whole thing eminently suited to country and climate.

The Spaniards were left undisturbed until 1806— nearly thirty years—until, surprisingly enough, they were visited by a Russian, the charming, good-looking, and most astute Nicolai Rezanov. In Russia, where he had served under Catherine the Great, Paul I and Alexander I, Rezanov was known as an immensely skillful and subtle administrator. He had visited Paris and made himself agreeable to Madame de Staël and, all in all, he was a highly civilized man of a kind never before seen in Yerba Buena.

Naturally enough Rezanov had other reasons behind his visit besides those of a friendly call on the Spaniards. He had obtained Czar Paul's signature to an instrument granting him dominion of the coast of northwest America for an ambitious trading project which, in view of Spanish-American feelings, he had tactfully renamed the Russian-American Fur Company. He and his trappers were in search of the skins of seals and sea otters, but when he sailed into the Bay and tried to begin negotiations he met with a firm refusal. He was told with immense politeness and courtesy, but with equal firmness, that the laws of Spain categorically forbade Spanish colonies from trading with foreign powers. The new colony of Yerba Buena could certainly not provide the first exception.

Rezanov would have failed completely in his mission if it had not been for the governor's daughter, a girl reported to be the most beautiful in California. To her, Rezanov seemed the most glamorous and handsome man she had ever seen. He was the familiar of emperors and accustomed to the fabulous glitter of the French court. He might, she dreamed, transform a simple Californian beauty into a grand lady of faraway Europe. Her dreams might have come true, for the charming Rezanov fell head over heels in love with her, and had it not been for differences of race and religion he would have married her on the spot. As it was the pair became engaged, and Rezanov sailed away from Yerba Buena, on what he hoped would be a temporary absence, with his ship's hold full of goods and with a

27

promise from the governor in his pocket that the proposed trading treaty would be forwarded to Spain for approval.

Unfortunately for Russia, Rezanov died of a fever within the year before anything had been accomplished. The Spaniards, once he had left, pursued the leisured pace of their tradition, and when news of the death of the "Russian Columbus" reached the beautiful fiancée he had left behind, she took the veil and retired into a convent. Rezanov's correspondence showed his clear intention of annexing the western coast to Russia and of encouraging immigration from his native land on a considerable scale. So the Peninsula, having escaped the English, might well have fallen into the hands of the Russians. But the only trace of that ambition today is the name Russian Hill which still exists in San Francisco.

During all those early years there was only one mention of earthquakes, but California's earthquake history is a long one, even though written records are short. It seems, however, impossible to believe that no shocks were felt after the first one recorded in 1769.

Then, in 1808, only two years after the visit of the fascinating Russians, comes the first earthquake entry for the San Francisco Bay area. The beautiful site declared itself unsafe from the attacks of the tremendous forces of the earth, and from then on there is an almost continuous earthquake history. Beauty in landscape is intimately connected with earthquakes; high mountains near broad oceans are often geologically treacherous while at the same time offering every kind of inducement for man to settle near them. If he does, it seems that he must put up with earthquakes.

A short twelve years after the earthquake of 1808 there was revolution in Mexico, and the Mexicans succeeded in turning out their Spanish masters. Two years later California agreed to give allegiance to Mexico in return for suitable representation in the Mexican Congress. Even so, life in Yerba Buena hardly changed; and that life continued peacefully Spanish in all but name. Mexico seemed very far away—as did the rest of the American continent, safely hidden behind the vast range of the Rocky Mountains. At that date American citizens were as much foreigners in California as were the British or the Russians.

But the peaceful, sunny Pacific peninsula had an irresistible fascination for the world outside. Seal and otter skins, the only furs that the place had to offer, were high fashion in the nineteenth century, and in 1836 the Hudson's Bay Company set up a trading post in Yerba Buena hoping, no doubt, to reap riches from their enterprise. Unluckily for the company, the inhabitants of that happy village still preserved the Spanish tradition of no trade with foreigners, and after five years the company abandoned their unprofitable business.

In the meantime America was steadily growing in power and it was becoming intolerable to her that Mexico should own her western coast and prevent its use for trade with the Far East. Nevertheless no action was taken until a man named John Charles Frémont, apparently on his own initiative, broke the peace and violated all international agreements by seizing some Mexican cavalry with the band of adventurers that he had collected around him. Frémont's men carried a very fine flag showing a bear—the same flag flown by the state of California today—and this they triumphantly raised, apparently with the intention of making the territory an independent state. Frémont's daring action forced America's hand, and when news of the declaration of war against Mexico in May 1846 reached California the army was already in possession of the northern part of the territory. By the peace treaty of February 1848 Upper California and New Mexico were ceded to America in return for a compensation of fifteen million dollars. In July 1848, one year after Yerba Buena had been renamed San Francisco, Captain John B. Montgomery arrived in the United States sloop of war *Portsmouth* and flew the Stars and Stripes in San Francisco in a plaza which is still called Portsmouth after his ship. Captain Frémont and his Bear Volunteers have been famous ever since. Among their memorials is the state flag of California.

The American Government must have known that its new territory had its own inherent dangers. In June 1836 there was a great earthquake in the San Francisco Bay area: fissures opened, and there was general havoc, although, owing to the small population—the whole area housed only about eight hundred people —there seems to have been no casualties. Two years later another severe earthquake occurred, this time on the San Francisco Peninsula itself. A great fissure opened which reached southward from the village to a point near Santa Clara. The shock cracked walls in the Presidio, badly injured walls at the Mission Dolores, and everywhere broke china and glassware.

It became apparent that colonizing California had its risks, but America had urgent reasons, which far outweighed the risks, for wishing to incorporate it as a state. For some time gold had been known to exist, and indeed had fairly frequently been found all over the area, but there had never been the slightest hint of a real bonanza until James Wilson Marshall, a native of New Jersey, made the long journey west on the Oregon Trail in January 1848 to build and operate a sawmill for a German named Sutter. One day, when Marshall happened to be standing some two hundred feet away from the completed mill, he noticed some glittering particles lodged on the bedrock channel of the swiftly flowing race. Some of these particles, he saw with amazement, were as large as grains of wheat. Marshall, normally a reserved and rather taciturn man, collected all the specimens he could lay hands on into the soft crown of his hat and rushed back to the mill crying: "Boys, I believe I've found a gold mine!"

He was right, and his find on that momentous Monday started the biggest gold rush in history. The hatful of stuff which Marshall had picked up that morning was found to be so rich that it seemed to promise that half the gold of the world was about to be found in California.

TWO

THE exciting news of Marshall's discovery of gold at Sutter's Mill in January 1848 was of enormous potential importance to America. But in those days the East was so far away from the West that it was not until August 19th that any news of it appeared in the eastern papers. Even then the "rumors" were received with a good deal of skepticism and with little interest by people as a whole. However, reports of a bonanza became more and more persistent, and in November the *New York Tribune* declared, "We are on the brink of the Age of Gold."

Despite this, President Polk delayed the official announcement of the find to Congress until the end of the year. His reason for such a delay is not clear, unless it was simple prudence. California was a long way from Washington, and conventional means of transportation were nonexistent. The territory was the newest baby of the federation, and had only been formally won over from Mexico in the preceding February. The President and his advisers knew that the news of the enormous find of gold would cause what might amount to a stampede, and it is possible that he wished to delay his official announcement until California had had a little more time to settle down as a member of the United States.

However, whatever Polk might choose to do, it was clearly impossible to stop the news from spreading once the *Tribune* had got hold of it and underwritten the truth of the wonderful rumors. All down the ages gold has held a unique fascination for man; color, texture and rarity are unparalleled, but apart from the undoubted physical attraction of the very metal itself it must always arouse feelings of cupidity and the promise of fortune. San Francisco, with its deep, safe bay, was the natural focus for would-be prospectors, and in a twinkling the little village with its eight hundred inhabitants and two hundred buildings was topsy-turvy with excitement. The whole territory rang with the cry of "Gold," and it seemed that the entire male population hurried off to prospect.

34

That was the beginning of the rush, but after the *Tribune*'s spread and the President's announcement, the whole world flocked to America's newly won territory. The place which formerly had been peopled by men so pleasantly unacquisitive as to torture a "Yankee conscience" was completely transformed, if not overnight, at least within a matter of months. The peak year of the gold rush was 1849, by which time news of the find was world-wide. Travelers from every nation headed for California and hopes of a fortune. To take but one example, so many Frenchmen arrived in San Francisco in those exciting days that they earned themselves a special nickname. Their ignorance of the English language, the tongue which, with the American possession, had quickly superseded Spanish on the Peninsula, obliged them to ask constantly, *"Qu'est-ce qu'il dit?"* And the rest of the laughing rip-roaring crowd christened the Frenchmen the "Keskydees" from the moment of their arrival.

But it was the Americans who arrived in the greatest numbers. Over on the eastern side of the continent business had been bad. Mortgages were heavy, and hard-pressed men saw a golden way to liquidate their debts if only they could make the three-thousand-mile journey west. It was not easy in 1849, as can be seen by anyone who flies over the territory today and takes the trouble to glance out of the window of his airplane. Once away from the

35

eastern seaboard, mile upon mile of flat and deserted Middle West country had to be crossed. It was all strange, unopened country to the Easterners. Roads were mere tracks, and hundreds of miles of desert or at least completely empty countryside lay ahead. Means of transport were nonexistent and men had to provide their own as best they could.

After the plains of the Middle West the enormous barrier of the Rocky Mountains rose before them; the promised land with all its richness of gold was still very far away. Land was barren and climate severe and the mountains seemed the highest in the world. Somehow or other the pioneers managed to cross the Rockies, only to meet another formidable barrier in the high Sierras, their peaks snow-covered even in summertime. But mountain ranges with uncharted roads did not deter the gold seekers. Some tried to cross the mountains, some came the long way round, some hiked, some traveled in wagons, some trundled wheelbarrows containing such personal belongings as they felt they could not leave behind. Altogether it was reckoned that forty thousand men passed through San Francisco in 1849.

Many men from Australia joined in the rush— that country to which Britain had sent the worst of her criminal population, many of whom duly arrived in San Francisco. The Australians set up a quarter of their own in the city, the notorious Sydney Town, where crimes of violence were a daily occurrence and where the night life began that was to gain such a sinister reputation for San Francisco. Many came around the terrible Cape Horn, by far the longest route, and the little sailing ships were often badly buffeted before they could turn that fearful promontory. Many ships were lost, but hundreds more lay in the Bay that fateful year. Some of the vessels in which the miners had traveled were so old and unseaworthy that they were left to rot, or were pulled up onto land to serve as shelters. For there were no houses for the great mass of the incoming throng, and though during that year they went up at the rate of from fifteen to thirty a day, they were mere shacks. People who had lived in comparative comfort in other parts of the world were compelled to live as they had never done before, without even the simplest necessities for a decent life.

Virtually no women went west in the gold rush, and the fame of the few who did has lived and grown into legend. One grandmother—and grandmothers seemed older in those days—was said to have made the journey and on arrival to have done her best to establish some sort of home comfort for her family, but she was a notable exception. Mrs. Mary Jane Megquier, whose letters have survived, was another. She and her husband had never got on very well in the East, and they decided at the last moment to undertake the long trail to California to make their fortune. Megquier was not conspicuously successful, but

37

his wife, who must have been a shrewd and hard-working businesswoman, hit on the idea of establishing a boardinghouse for lonely miners. Naturally enough she had plenty of customers and her house, when she got it, was always crammed to capacity.

During the early years the population of San Francisco was certainly nine-tenths male, and the excitement caused by the arrival of any female was intense. One night, for example, a musket was discharged in the camps to signal the arrival of a woman, and immediately a crowd of men went along just to get a sight of her. "Stranger," they said to her embarrassed husband, "we have understood that our mothers were women, but it is so long since we have seen them that we have forgotten how a woman looks, and, being told you have caught one, we are prospecting to get a glimpse."

Saloons were full of men and dance halls were crowded with men dancing together, the rough rule being that those with brightly colored patches on their pants should dance the woman's part.

Among the immigrants was the famous Mormon Samuel Brannan. He had been sent to San Francisco by his leader, Brigham Young, to prospect not for gold, but for a suitable site for the establishment of a Mormon city. Unfortunately for his faith, he and his band found themselves caught up in the gold rush, and it was not very long before Brannan caught the fever, forgot his message and went out prospecting for gold instead of souls. He grew rich and famous and the Mormon town was established in Salt Lake City instead of in San Francisco, and without any help from him.

The shantytown of the gold rush lived fast and furiously. Many of the men who flocked to San Francisco never intended to stay there. Their idea was to get rich quick and clear out home again, and not for the first or last time the normal standards of decent people were corrupted by the idea of impermanence. But in spite of the slackening off of the fabulous stream of gold in the year 1850, many of the pioneers stayed on. The western part of America was beginning to open up in earnest, and, second only to the gold of California, the silver mines of Nevada later promised wealth to prospectors. Houses in San Francisco continued to go up at a fabulous rate— many of them arriving in the Bay prefabricated from the Far East. Chinese and others saw to it that there was plenty to buy in the newly opened shops, and in 1860, with the population (which in 1848 was 800) up to 40,000, trade was brisk.

Women were still in a small minority in that prosperous, hard-living, roistering city, and entrepreneurs were not slow in seizing the opportunity to get rich. Thus the Barbary Coast was born—that name which should have conjured up a picture of a savage shore, pirates, and high adventure—almost anything, in fact, except a block or two in a modern American city. No one could ever tell exactly how the name originated, but the pirates were certainly there, ready for any unfortunate sailor or prospector with a pocketful of money. They were not dressed in swashbuckling knee breeches and silken sashes—in fact the pirates of the San Francisco Barbary Coast were hardly dressed at all—but in their way they were as dangerous as their marine counterparts. Trade in "amusement" was brisker and more gaudy than any other form of commerce in the city. The *Call* described it well:

Barbary Coast! That mysterious region so much talked of, so seldom visited! . . . That sink of moral pollution, whose reefs are strewn with human wrecks, and into whose vortex go the sinking hulks of the murdered and the suicide! . . . Night is the time to visit the Coast. In the daytime it is dull and unattractive . . . but when night lets fall its dusky curtain, the Coast brightens into life, and becomes the wild carnival of crime . . . that bursts forth with energy renewed by its siesta.

Saloons as well as dance halls (most of them in cellars) were used for dancing, while the melodeons—the name came from a small reed organ with which each was originally equipped—offered entertainment for men only. Some of the melodeons were "superior" places where prostitutes seldom appeared in public. Semiprofessional performers were engaged for the concerts given there, and some of them later became outstanding vaudeville stars of the American stage. Female performers sold drinks in the intervals and made what profit they could in the curtained boxes which were a feature of the houses. The Bella Union was probably the most famous of these superior melodeons, and young bloods of San Francisco went there to get a taste of life in the raw. Every sort of mechanical musical instrument was installed and could be operated for a nickel or a dime, and many of these old machines are on view, still workable, in San Francisco today.

The lowest type of "deadfall," as the places were popularly called, often employed from ten to fifty females, some as young as twelve or fourteen, some old and toothless but attractive because of their experience. All were known as "pretty waiter-girls," regardless of age; all wore calculatedly scanty costumes. But if a customer did not think he was getting his money's worth he was permitted for a small extra charge to strip any girl he desired. The pretty waiter-girls received wages of from fifteen to twenty-five dollars a week plus commission on the amount of liquor they sold to their customers—a commission which greatly increased their earnings. Liquor always gurgled and flowed like ice water from a tap. Miners and sailors were thirsty, and money was plentiful on the Barbary Coast: without money no visitor was welcome.

41

Performers at the "concerts" in the lower types of dive were not as a rule talented; sometimes, indeed, they were extremely comical just because they were enormously ungainly. The woman known as the "Galloping Cow" was a typical example, but she wisely saved all the money she earned by entertainment—whether prostitution or otherwise—and ultimately became respectable in an establishment of her own.

Drugs and aphrodisiacs were used if a man was stubborn. Then the pretty waiter-girls could be trusted not to let him go until his wallet was empty, and in all probability he was put outside and rolled into the gutter as an end to his evening's entertainment. If a man was reasonably generous and suitably amorous he was mulcted of considerable sums of money, but he probably enjoyed himself and came back for more on his next visit to San Francisco.

The most depraved of the dives did not even bother to curtain their windows, so that whatever went on in the brothels was visible to anyone passing in the street—no doubt in the hope of attracting more custom. The press of San Francisco was loud in its condemnation of these degrading practices, but the police, though they always walked about the blocks in couples, seemed unable or unwilling to exercise any restraint upon the dens beyond ordering in one case that the women instead of being naked above the waist should wear thin blouses.

The cribs, the parlor houses, and such famous places as the Eureka and the Strassburg Music Hall, the latter operated by Spanish Kitty who ultimately retired with a fortune, all had red lights over their doors and were famous throughout America. They undoubtedly exercised a great influence upon the dancing habits of the continent, and in them originated dance steps taught by dancing masters all over the world.

Gold made (or ruined) San Francisco. It turned the place from a small gentle village with a few peaceful inhabitants into a violent and vicious city. It created the notorious Barbary Coast, swamped it with thousands of men of all nations who owed the city no allegiance and were simply concerned with getting rich if they could and taking pleasure where they conveniently found it. There was money to spend, and apart from the politely named cribs San Francisco was a natural for gambling houses which became famous throughout the continent.

But prosperity, however remarkable, and men, however rich, could not alter the fact that the city was in earthquake country. Everybody knew it, most had experienced a shock or two, but equally, nearly everyone preferred to ignore the danger. Citizens so newly arrived as hardly to merit the name were so much concerned with the business of making their fortunes easily and hurriedly that they paid scant attention to anything that did not directly con-

43

cern their object. The business of getting rich quick was all they thought of.

In the official *Descriptive Catalogue of the Earthquakes of the Pacific Coast*, many hundreds of earthquakes, not including the uncounted aftershocks, are plainly listed; and it can only be assumed that people either became used to them or refused to notice them in those mad gold-hunting days. As the majority of buildings in the new city were temporary, damage was not considered important. If there were casualties in an earthquake—as surely there must have been—human life was cheap, nearly everyone was a foreigner without any family in San Francisco, so why worry?

The San Andreas and Hayward faults from which the main earthquake danger sprang, though they were not yet properly mapped, were clearly known in the nineteenth century. The former, which most nearly affected San Francisco (although the city could also suffer from a movement of the Hayward fault), is an old fracture of the earth's crust running from Cape Mendocino to the Colorado desert—a distance of some six hundred miles. In the San Francisco area it runs from Tomales Bluff (lying northwest of the city) through the pretty inlet of Inverness, where the narrow water is covered with boats today, through the village of Olema and under Stinson Beach (one of the pleasure spots of Marin County), to pass under the Pacific Ocean at

44

the Golden Gate. The fault re-enters the land again at Mussel Rock, west of Colma, and runs southeastward down the Peninsula, where long, straight, narrow ponds or lakes mark its path until it reaches Crystal Springs, San Francisco's reservoir. The city itself, therefore, is not directly over the fault, though near enough to suffer severely should it move in an earthquake. The country through which the San Andreas fault passes is, like much earthquake country, charming and serene to look at. It is for the most part particularly well-wooded, and nothing could look less alarming or more peaceful. It is almost impossible to imagine the danger that lies beneath, and for a long time San Francisco preferred not to try.

It is not easy to understand exactly why faults give way. Is it the result of strains and stresses underneath the surface crust of the earth, the upper part of which is only forty miles thick? Forty miles down sounds deep enough until it is realized that the whole length of the fault itself in the immediate San Francisco area—a comfortable half day's motoring— is about double that distance. But *seven hundred* miles down through the crust is a center composed, roughly speaking, of a ball of metal, mainly of iron, but with a proportion of nickel and other metals in it. Surrounding the center is a lower layer of crust which must certainly be intensely hot, but which is plastic rather than molten, being kept so

45

by the pressure of the top crust above it—a crust consisting of solid rock and therefore very heavy. If that pressure is relieved even to a small extent the underlying material may actually become molten and liquid so that it moves and seeks to find some way of escape. The perfect way of escape is, of course, through a fault or crack in the surface rock where the formation has once been broken down and remains weaker than the rest of the earth's crust. When, therefore, the plastic layer deep down in the earth becomes for one reason or another molten, it will seek and find escape through just such an outlet as the San Andreas fault with a resulting earthquake shock as the fault creeps or moves under the enormous strain below.

Ironically enough, the wonderful California climate adds its own earthquake dangers to those which already exist in the presence of the two great faults. Along the beautiful coastal ranges of that lovely country (which perhaps even now is not completely settled in its final geological form) the rock faces are covered with a layer of soil and decomposed stone which year by year accumulates faster than the winter rains, however severe, can remove it. During the long dry summers, when for months on end there is no rain at all, the surface shrinks and cracks to a considerable depth, allowing easy access to torrential downpours when they occur. The water penetrates the loose deposit, making it plastic and at the same time very heavy—splendid raw material for a vast earth slump easily set in motion by an earthquake.

Throughout history earthquakes and fires have been intimately connected. From 1849, when the miners came to San Francisco, the city suffered a series of great fires which, though they never seem to have been officially connected with earthquakes, were nevertheless most destructive and alarming for the population. The pattern throughout those years was one of a series of conflagrations, enormous damage, feverish rebuilding, and then some fresh conflagration to destroy most of what had been built up.

The great fire of 1849 destroyed a million dollars' worth of property in the city, but in four months the whole ramshackle, untidy place was rebuilt after a fashion. That feverish rebuilding was typical of San Francisco. From the beginning it was designed—if design it could be called—to be a success city, and nothing and nobody should stop it. The newly arrived citizens were ebullient, energetic, and optimistic—qualities which survive in San Francisco today. But their rebuilt paradise only survived for a month, for on May 4, 1850, a second great fire devastated the city. In June there was another outbreak, this time in a different location. At that time the summer breezes which keep San Francisco cool under the heat of the sun were at full strength and it was

47

quite impossible to stop the fire. But once more the citizens refused to be beaten: "When the fiery meal was done the citizens cleared away the rubbish and set a new meal more tempting than before." It was soon eaten, for a bare three months later, in September, the enemy struck again. Cries of "Fire!" aroused sleepers in the middle of the night, causing such terror and alarm as could hardly be matched in any other city in the world. Four terrible fires in eight months left a feeling of acute apprehension in the minds of thoughtful people. Nights were gay as ever on the Barbary Coast; dancing and gambling went on till dawn. But the civic authorities were afraid and very anxious about the safety of their city. It was common talk that a gang of desperadoes had sworn to keep the anniversary of each conflagration by starting one that might be yet more serious. If this was true, and if in addition there was an ever-present danger of earthquakes, there seemed to be no end to the danger from fire.

The alleged fire-raisers were probably the same as the gangs of street arabs—to use the nineteenth-century word—who made the Chinese population of San Francisco their special target and came to be known as "hoodlums"—thus having the honor of adding an important word to the American language. The origin of the name is not clear, but a likely story has it that it came from the gang leader Muldoon whose name pronounced in reverse, probably as a sort of disguise, was Noodlum, and thence, by a miswriting of the initial letter, Hoodlum. The other and less picturesque explanation is that the gang call was "huddle 'em," which was in time contracted to "hoodlum." In any case the name was certainly used in the late nineteenth century in San Francisco to designate gangs of thieves and bad boys who preyed upon the population, and it has proved itself only too useful ever since.

If the fire-raisers were the same gangs as those who set out to persecute the Chinese, they had a wonderful opportunity in San Francisco's Chinatown, where every building above ground was flimsy enough to burn well and quickly. The place was a famous feature of the up-and-coming city. It was started, so it was said, by two men and a woman, subjects of the Son of Heaven, who slipped into early San Francisco and for a time were lost to sight. The three were quickly followed by a flood of Chinese all making for the gold fields, and at the end of the century there were probably some 35,000 of them in the state. But the Chinese, as it turned out, were not very successful miners, and before long many of them returned to work in San Francisco itself. With its enormously increased population it presented excellent opportunities for private enterprise in business, and very soon the Chinese set themselves up in such occupations as laundry work, personal service to residents, and manual labor of all kinds. With most other able-

49

bodied men occupied in the search for gold, the Orientals were very useful. In addition Chinatown became an attraction for tourists. The narrow streets were filled with a shuffling throng of blue-bloused yellow men, and little shops displayed beautiful silks, embroideries, and novelties. Large potbellied lanterns, red with strange lettering, swung from balconies; yellow and vermilion strips of paper, bearing strange symbols, were pasted on lintels; and there was a curious mingling of odors, a smell of musk and incense, stale tobacco and plain dirt. American visitors found the place fascinating. Having never been to the Orient they enjoyed finding it in San Francisco.

Chinatown was not merely a tourist's paradise; it had a very ugly side to it. Drugs, gambling, slave prostitutes—all these abounded in that narrow quarter of San Francisco. The Chinese girls, pretty and attractive to men of any race, were freely brought in through Canadian ports, often traveling in padded crates labeled FREIGHT to conform with the law. Some of the girls, such as the famous "golden girls" Ah Toy and Selina, lived in expensive brothels or "parlor cribs," as they were called, sumptuously furnished with cushions and silken hangings and scented with clouds of incense. Their charms were naturally rated much higher than those of the girls in the commoner cribs, which were small one-storied shacks divided into two by curtains and sometimes occupied by as many as six prostitutes. The only door to the shacks had a small barred window in front of which the girls stood to attract the attention of potential customers. Their soft, strange cry of "China girl nice! You come inside please" was very successful, and until early morning the plaintive, Oriental voices of the crib girls could be heard crying in a monotonous singsong: "Two bittee lookee, flo bittee feelee, six bittee does." But, golden girls or not, they were all slaves, and their price (generally $250) was included in bills of sale among such items as rice, shrimps, and salt fish. They had almost all been kidnaped and doped in China, and awakened, utterly at the mercy of their masters, in San Francisco.

Prostitution in Chinatown did not seem to worry the authorities nearly as much as what went on in the Barbary Coast section. Presumably it offered fewer problems, for whereas the Coast girls were white Americans, the inhabitants of Chinatown, both masters and slaves, were aliens conscious of their precarious position and only too anxious to keep out of trouble.

There was, nevertheless, great opposition to the Chinese in the city, though it was not wholly connected with the dark goings-on in the cribs of Chinatown. The truth was that the Oriental traders were suddenly found to be much too well organized among themselves to please their American hosts. Their existence, it was felt, was a serious menace to legitimate American business, for the rich Chinese merchants had banded themselves together so effectively that they dominated every business enterprise in Chinatown, as well as some outside its limits. Their organization was called the Six Companies, and they advanced money to those of their countrymen who wished to emigrate to the United States, paid their passages, found them jobs, and thereafter saw to it not only that the loan was repaid with interest, but also that they received a portion of the immigrant's wages so long as he remained in America.

The flimsy prefabricated dwellings of Chinatown were matched below ground by cellars in which hundreds lived together in a squalor perhaps slightly less than they had been accustomed to in China, but shocking by western standards even in San Francisco, itself so lately a shantytown. The Chinese cellars were the talk of the city and were known variously as the Devil's Kitchen, the Dog Kennel, the Ragpickers' Alley, and—in a climax of facetiousness—the Palace Hotel. In spite of a rather furtive interest in their dark doings taken by San Franciscans, the Chinese were subjected to a good deal of persecution and, if it had not been for friendly police not averse from taking a bribe, the whole structure might well have collapsed. For it was not only teenage gangs who harried them. There were many rep-

resentations in high quarters about their dangerous practices and, above all, about the steady
increase in the Oriental population in San Francisco. American businessmen feared the competition of the Chinese, and during his term of office
President Grant consented to receive the report of a
special committee on the subject. Naturally enough
the report unanimously condemned the Orientals,
whether Chinese or Japanese, and demanded protection from them.

So seriously did the report of the committee to the
President seem to endanger their livelihood and their
very existence in America that the Six Companies
were at length obliged to break the customary im-
penetrable reserve of their race and submit a memorial to the President in their own defense. The
memorial was presented with characteristic Chinese
dignity and propriety and spoke for all the yellow
people of San Francisco. The Six Companies admitted
frankly that they were aware that a number of Chinese women prostitutes had been brought into the city
by the yellow men, but alleged that at first these were
brought from China "at the wish and for the gratifica-
tion of white men." No one who knew anything of the
life that went on in the Barbary Coast could doubt
the truth of their assertion. But they added that
"if officers would refuse bribes, then unprincipled
Chinamen could no longer purchase immunity from
the punishment of their crimes."

Though possibly not entirely ingenuous, the memorial presented to the President was historic because it was the first attempt made by the large Oriental population of the West to justify their existence as citizens. It set out at some length a case that was virtually unanswerable, and in time San Franciscans had to admit that on the whole the Chinese were a sober and industrious section of the population. Persecution died down, and the yellow men were tolerated provided that Chinatown did not spread over the city and that no further mass invasions could ever take place.

THREE

IN the years immediately following the gold rush there was plenty of gold in San Francisco but a great shortage of actual coins. In the mining districts gold *dust* was in circulation right up until 1856, and all sorts of bargains were made by men who wanted goods but had no actual money with which to pay for them. The owner of a general goods store—a primitive affair little more than a tent— would be only too glad to accept gold, and a careless man might be seen offering a handful of the precious stuff weighing, perhaps, up to one and a half ounces for a packet of Seidlitz powders. The storekeeper grew rich and his customers were satisfied, and so no one at first worried much about the lack of actual dollars.

But in the city itself it was obviously impossible to continue such rough and ready practices. A man could not carry a weighing machine around with him and was generally reluctant to trust the storekeeper to weigh his hard-won dust exactly, so that the problem of cash became acute. The Federal Mint in Philadelphia was three thousand miles away and impossibly difficult of access from San Francisco in those early days when transportation across the Middle West and over the mountains was practically nonexistent. Men who grew rich fast wanted to spend fast as well; they could not be expected to wait until enough American dollars arrived to meet their need. All sorts of money, British, French, Spanish and German, circulated freely and were freely accepted when the miners first came to the West.

But the obvious answer to the currency problem lay in private mints, and these were quickly set up by men who saw in them a means of profiting by the bonanza and who were clever enough to acquire the technical skill required for minting coins. They issued gold pieces of large denominations—five-, ten- and twenty-dollar coins—which suited the needs of large business transactions. Curiously enough, the private mintmasters chose to issue many octagonal coins (they survive today, though they are very rare) and on some of them they put Indian designs such as the famous Indian Chief and Indian Princess. But in 1851 Congress agreed to set up a Federal Mint in San Francisco itself, and as a guarantee of good faith issued a fifty-dollar piece from the assay office in the city. The private mints were at once out of business as far as the large denominations were concerned. But now San Franciscans needed small change, not (as in the East) in copper, nickel or small silver, but in their own beloved gold. So little "spangles" of quarter and half dollars appeared and also, later on, the first one-dollar pieces to be issued in the West. When the San Francisco Mint started operations in earnest (which, in spite of the decree of Congress, was not until 1854) all other coins except those issued from its official dies were gradually forced out of circulation and became collectors' pieces of increasing rarity and value.

All through the second part of the century San Francisco grew at an amazing speed and the population grew with (and often outstripped) the building. There was such progress in the city of the West as few parts of the world had ever seen. But it was a hazardous city; savage outbreaks of fire still occurred with alarming frequency, and before long another danger began to appear. In the year 1853 several newly erected buildings fell down, including the United States Bonded Warehouse at the corner of Union and Battery Streets. This particular in-

57

cident was only one of several of like nature, and the reason for their fall was not far to seek. Even in the most elegant houses in the city, inferior building materials were generally used; and it was publicly acknowledged that such materials could not resist the strain put upon them by shifting and treacherous foundations caused by the increasing area of filled ground. The natural site of the city at the end of the Peninsula was narrow. Real estate men thus came more and more to rely on the practice of reclaiming land from the shallow part of the sea bed along the vast waterfront. There was an enormous demand for land on which to build houses and warehouses, and this encroachment upon the sea seemed a heaven-sent answer. Waste and trash, packing cases, garbage, and every sort of suitable and unsuitable material was used to build up the land. A thin coating of sand and earth was then laid upon it, and the sites were ready for building. But the resistance of such sites was negligible when there was any movement of the faults, and foundations could hardly fail to be insecure. In addition to the danger of using filled ground, there was a high confidence abroad in the prosperous city which seemed to justify the abandonment of the old policy of allowing only low buildings to go up. Toward the end of the nineteenth century the authorities allowed many-storied offices to be built on the new

American skyscraper pattern. They were not, of course, comparable with those of Manhattan, but they were too high to be safe for San Francisco at a time before modern building techniques had been perfected. If it was generally acknowledged that buildings fell because of shifting foundations and poor materials, the outlook—once the skyscraper policy had been allowed—was far from promising.

In October 1853 there was another great fire in which the popular old Saint Francis Hotel, which had escaped all previous conflagrations unscathed, was destroyed. The Saint Francis was typical of old San Francisco—shoddily built yet always gay with the most fashionable and liveliest spirits of the city. It was said that the bedrooms were separated from one another by such thin partitions that everything that was being said and done next door could be heard—and that included much that should never have been heard at all. With all its aristocratic pretension, bedrooms at the Saint Francis gave rise to more tales of scandal and more incidents guaranteed to raise a laugh in the clubs and bars than any other building in the city. When it caught fire the new and splendid Fire Force performed prodigies of daring in the attempt to save it, but without avail. But San Francisco did not care; even though there was no insurance in those days the Saint Francis was rebuilt in a matter of months and quickly resumed its important place in society.

The last great conflagration of the nineteenth century was in May 1854. May is apt to be a windy month in San Francisco, and had the wind been stronger that day the greater part of the place must have perished. "About this period of the year," wrote one of the chroniclers of the city, "those high winds fairly set in which fan flames to their height and suddenly communicate them to new materials across wide empty spaces and streets notwithstanding all the unwearied exertions of perhaps the bravest and most skillful set of firemen in the world." That account might well stand for a short and detached description of the later, most famous fire of them all. In this fire of 1854 enormous numbers of wooden houses were destroyed, including those built from the native redwood which in the past had been found to be far more fire-resistant than any other kind. In that year, too, the practice of blowing up buildings to prevent the spread of fire was widely used; backfires were started and all known anti-fire devices used, but with little effect. There was no word of an earthquake, either to account for the collapse of buildings or the starting of the fire. Indeed, no one seemed to bother very much about causes in those early days. Collapse and conflagration came and went and the only thing to do was to rebuild, as fast as possible, such parts of the city as had been ruined so that the citizens might get on with the business of making fortunes quickly and easily.

60

The records of nineteenth-century earthquakes are scanty, and many must have gone unrecorded, but it is known that in the years 1857, 1865, and 1890 there were shocks, the origin of which could be directly traced to the San Andreas fault. In 1868 there was an earthquake connected equally with the Hayward fault, on the eastern side of the Bay. The fault runs parallel to the San Andreas fault and is about eighteen and a half miles away from it. Thus the city of San Francisco, though nearer to the San Andreas than to the Hayward fault, is not directly over either of them. Yet in the earthquake of 1868 the city suffered considerable damage, particularly on filled ground, and many fires broke out. But the authorities congratulated themselves on their Fire Force, for there was plenty of water and the skill of the firemen soon had everything under control.

The occurrence of the 1868 earthquake is very interesting, for it undoubtedly gave San Francisco confidence that their city would never again be seriously menaced by a conflagration. Yet if the facts are examined the fallacy is clear. The 1868 earthquake was directly connected with the Hayward fault, and although it is farther from the city than the San Andreas fault there was much damage as well as an outbreak of fire. But it was the San Andreas fault that constituted by far the graver danger to the city, and when the time came to pipe a water supply into San Francisco the pipes were laid along a course that crossed right over that fault line. The water company was privately owned, and thirty-inch mains fed many local storage cisterns, which were connected in turn to private houses as well as to the hydrants—a thing which would never be tolerated today because of the obvious dangers in an emergency. No one asked what would happen to the San Francisco water supply if the San Andreas fault moved and the mains were cracked by the movement, as they were almost bound to be. But it was a relevant question, and it was only answered at the beginning of the twentieth century. If the danger inherent in the location of the water mains had ever occurred to the city authorities they might have developed the possibility of using sea water from the Bay as a possible alternative to mains water in case of fire. Such a project would, of course, have necessitated special equipment and a considerable expenditure of money, for salt is a corrosive and the city's ordinary hose pipes would have been useless. But, if it had been seriously considered, there were plenty of men in San Francisco with brains good enough to solve the problem of using salt water; and there was certainly no lack of money with which to finance the undertaking.

The chief of the Fire Force was always something of a hero in San Francisco. In 1906 the man in command was Danny Sullivan who, because of his outstanding ability, his wisdom, and his personal character, became the idol of the city. Sullivan was not a strong man, and after a while his doctors warned him that he must take things more easily. On that account he built a house by the ocean for himself and his wife where he could go to relax whenever his duties allowed. Sullivan thought that a career in the Fire Force was about the best thing in the world for a young man, and he was always on the lookout for suitable recruits. While living down at his house on the beach he made it his business to get to know the young men of the neighborhood, one of whom was named Rudi Schubert, a boy who had joined the Coastal Life Guards after he gave up going to sea, and was now thinking of getting married. Schubert and his friends often went for rides in Sullivan's buggy down on the coast in their spare time, and a warm friendship, almost amounting to hero worship, grew up between the men. Schubert needed little persuading that he would have a much better career in the Fire Force than he could ever hope for in the Life Guards. Certainly after he joined up he had his full share of excitement.

Unfortunately Danny Sullivan was not as successful in persuading the city authorities to listen to him when he warned them that, in spite of what they thought were adequate precautions, the city in his opinion was far from safe if there should be a severe outbreak of fire. "I do feel sometimes," he said, "that dangers beset us daily of which the great masses know little or nothing. To contend with fire is my life's work, so it is only natural that I should think of such things."

He urged not only thorough training in dynamiting for his men, but also a proper investigation of the city's water supply, which he considered wholly inadequate for the task that might one day face the fire fighters. He constantly pleaded with the authorities for a proper plant for utilizing the salt water of the Bay in case of fire. It was a scheme that had been proposed and rejected before; Sullivan knew as well as any man what it would involve, but he considered it vitally necessary to the safety of San Francisco. But, though the city loved and revered its fire chief, nobody listened to him. Life was so enjoyable and everyone was so busy making money that it seemed a waste of time to worry about disaster. Everyone knew what earthquakes felt like, but they were disposed to joke about them. There had been many shocks, it was true, but nothing very serious had ever happened. Why should it happen now? So when Sullivan spoke of an inadequate water supply and geologists talked of the San Andreas fault no one was inclined to pay very much attention. Their reason, as a sixteenth-century writer said of the court of France, "was almost extinguished by the great love of pleasure, as a river is choked by mud.''

Earth's resentment at the mockery of San Franciscans, or perhaps its sardonic amusement at the capers of little men upon its surface, was a long time in making itself felt. Its force was boundless, but it was content to bide its time. With so many precautions neglected, so much proud fortune hunting, and so little forethought, it was inevitable that the ground should have the last word in the early San Francisco story. With one convulsive movement it could ruin the city and utterly destroy all that had been built up in the feverish quest for fortune.

In 1906 the population of San Francisco was about 450,000. Progress such as few cities had ever known had been made there since the miners came in '49. The gold rush was over long ago, but business was booming and there were many millionaires in the beautiful houses on Nob Hill—houses which today are gone save for one magnificent example which astonishes by its size and appearance. Famous San Franciscans also lived in the palaces on Van Ness Avenue, and the names Flood, Crocker, Huntington, Spreckels, Hopkins, Green, Scott, De Young and many more were household words. In addition to the money kings there were people who though not rich were famous. The world traveler Jack London was born in the city and always loved it, and to name but one other the widow of the famous English author Robert Louis Stevenson had a house on Nob Hill. San Francisco with its wonderful climate, its many theatres, its clubs and its opera was one of the pleasantest places in the world in which to live.

It was perhaps natural that a city that contained two such famous pleasure quarters as the Barbary Coast and Chinatown should acquire the name of being the "friskiest" and the most vicious in all America. Prostitution, debauchery, girl slaves, and all kinds of unmentionable practices were believed to go on in the legendary parts of the town and, though rumor probably exaggerated, there was certainly a good deal of truth in what was generally said. Among the "respectable" population gambling, and especially the game of faro, was a major diversion. All the men gambled, and stakes in that rich city were apt to be very high with enormous consequent losses. Perhaps the most famous story of the time is that of the man of considerable fortune and position who played night after night at the faro table, losing continuously, and always trying to win back what he had lost. At last, so it was said, having no more money, he staked his fine house and all it contained on one final, spectacular and desperate bid. But his luck did not turn and he lost again; there was nothing left for him but to go home and tell his wife that their home had gone and that they must leave San Francisco forever.

From time to time campaigns were initiated to

66

try to clean up the city, but nothing very much was ever accomplished. To serious reformers it seemed as though the citizens must have a perverse pride in the highly colored reputation of the town that was said to be extreme in both virtue and in vice. Certainly the reformers can hardly have had much help from the municipal authorities, for in 1906 Eugene Schmitz, a man of most doubtful reputation, was elected Mayor of San Francisco for the third time. Schmitz was a tall, athletic-looking man of German and Irish descent whose chief virtue was that he was on the whole popular with the labor force —a thing vital to the business interests in the city. He was an interesting man, for in addition to a forceful personality he had artistic ability, being an accomplished violinist and president of the Musicians' Union of San Francisco. But honorable men, talking among themselves in the hotels and meeting places of the city, said that if ever the town should be in danger the Mayor, like Nero, would still be found fiddling, and not only on the violin. He was strongly suspected of graft and in 1908 was to be actually convicted, narrowly escaping a prison sentence. The city, known for its vicious and dangerous quarters, was in the hands of a man who was distrusted by the citizens as a whole and whose leadership was suspect. It was a curious situation for a place whose motto was "Pride, peace and progress," and one not likely to improve its reputation or to build up an atmosphere of confidence in San Francisco itself. Not that, in general, people worried much about possible graft in the city's administration. It was an "arrogant, upward reaching" time. Prosperity and riches with their attendant pleasures seemed enough, and the unpleasant word "cupidity" was ignored by common consent. So, too, was the substructure of permanent contentment, and the small quiet ways of caution; too little attention was paid, amid the general wellbeing, to wise geological warnings; and in the end San Francisco suffered a greater catastrophe than could have been conceived possible.

In the early hours of Wednesday, April 18, 1906, the skyscraper offices of the *Call,* one of the city's most famous landmarks, were as usual humming with last preparations for the late edition of the morning paper.

Easter was just over, and San Francisco was preparing for a renewal of its accustomed gaieties after the slight curb put upon them by Lent. The omens were good, for the Metropolitan Opera Company of New York was in town and had given a first performance, with Olive Fremstad, on Monday night. But that had been only a foretaste of the delights to come later in the week. On Tuesday Caruso, the most famous tenor in the world, had taken the role of Don José in *Carmen*. His name alone would have filled the opera house, but he had with him the great *basso* Rossi and the popular Scotti, supported by the finest company in America. San Francisco was prepared for a musical treat and a crowd of visitors from out of town had arrived for the first performance of *Carmen.* Hotels, including of course the fabulous Palace, owned by William Sharon after the presumed suicide (by swimming out to sea) of his partner William Ralston, were full to capacity.

The Palace Hotel had been the subject of what can only be called legendary exaggeration. It was said that a contract had been signed to conduct the waters of the beautiful Bridal Veil waterfall all the way from Yosemite Valley to San Francisco, so that it could pour perpetually over the west front of the hotel in a splendid, man-made cascade. Equally the beds were, so it was declared, to be made entirely of Swiss watch springs—the finest in the world—and stuffed with camel's hair, each hair to cost eleven cents! Another story was that there were to be thirty-four elevators in the building, four for passengers, ten for baggage, and twenty to carry mixed drinks up to the luxurious suites. Each elevator would, so rumor had it, contain a piano and a bowling alley. This was all, of course, an amusing myth; but the Palace did cost $4,000,000, and it was so sumptuous that it boasted of being one of the wonders of the continent. To complete the luxury offered to guests it had at one time a glass-roofed courtyard into which visitors could drive in their carriages without risk of getting wet as they alighted.

Gay parties had filled every restaurant on the evening of April 17th, and the streets were thronged with carriages and even a few automobiles carrying smartly dressed and wealthy people to meet their friends before going on to the opera.

But the *Call*'s headlines prepared for Wednesday morning showed that San Francisco was interested in many other things besides night life. The headlines speak for themselves:

MORGAN'S PARTNER RUN IN FOR DRIVING
WRONG SIDE OF THE STREET
MAXIM GORKY SAYS YANKEES ARE
SPITTERS
MYRIADS OF DIVORCES INVALIDATED BY
SUPREME COURT VERDICT
FREAK STORM IN OLD SHASTA—
PEOPLE ARE SCARED
CLERGYMAN FOR CHARGE OF HERESY

In addition, the recent eruption of Vesuvius made front-page news. A fund had been raised in the city for the victims, and on that April morning the *Examiner* announced the fine total of $23,000. Everyone in San Francisco knew what an earthquake was like—after all, their own city had been damaged from time to time, even if only slightly. Practical sympathy would always be forthcoming for that kind of trouble.

But the performance at the opera the night before was the most interesting news of the day, and papers gave much space to descriptions of dresses and of the elegant ladies wearing them: MANY BRILLIANT GOWNS ADD TO CHARM OF OPERA was a headline that took its place alongside CARUSO MAKES DON JOSÉ THE LEADING ROLE and CARUSO ALL THAT SAVED CARMEN. Possibly the Metropolitan Opera Company might not have been too pleased with San Francisco's press comments on its performance. But the cast probably never saw them. Those late editions were destined to an oblivion that could never have been anticipated, and not for a very long time afterward did any of the papers carry comparable headlines.

FOUR

THE dawn of Wednesday, April 18th, broke serene. The brilliant California sun early began to chase away the fog and mist that had shrouded the city overnight, and the little fresh wind so characteristic of San Francisco gave promise of a delightful day for the crowded city.

Unlike hurricanes, earthquakes give no warning to those they are about to ruin. There is no such thing as earthquake weather—no sudden rise in temperature, no high wind, no thunder, no far-off rumbling. There is nothing, either physical or psychological, to cause feelings of suspense or alarm before the actual shock occurs.

72

At five o'clock in the morning the streets of San Francisco were quiet and very nearly empty. The only people abroad were one or two policemen on their beat, some journalists leaving their offices after their night's work was done, a few workmen going early to work, and milkmen beginning to deliver the morning's milk in the city. And naturally enough in San Francisco there were also parties of revelers who had been out all night enjoying themselves and who were returning home, still in evening dress.

Everything seemed completely normal in the modern, prosperous city of the West. But at five hours, twelve minutes, and thirty-eight seconds the famous clock that surmounted the Ferry Building on the waterfront stopped abruptly.

The earth, apparently so comfortably solid and friendly, showed itself the savage enemy of those who had built their homes and lives upon it. For nearly the whole of an awful minute there was a noise like a broadside from all the guns of hell. It lasted only a very short time—less than a third of the time it takes to boil an egg—but it seemed like eternity.

The terrible noise was accompanied by a rocking of the whole city. San Francisco was shaken as a terrier shakes a rat. The motion was fantastic, at first horizontal, then, as waves came in from more distant parts, coalescing into the most extraordinary twists. Chimneys and spires were snapped off

73

as though from the lash of a whip; brick walls were crumbled and feeble buildings crushed like eggshells. Open fissures appeared near the wharves along the magnificent waterfront. In that quarter, ground had been artificially made up for building and there earth waves two or three feet high appeared and undulated through the ground. These waves were like nothing so much as those of the Pacific Ocean that beat forever along the rocky coast outside the shelter of the Golden Gate and which until then had seemed so much more dreadful and menacing than any "solid" earth could ever be. Floors trembled, whole buildings rocked, and it seemed as though the world were crashing to its end.

The first shock lasted only thirty seconds. When it was over, San Franciscans thought all danger was past. After all, they were accustomed to repeated tremors. But after ten seconds of quiet the second shock, worse than the first, more vigorous and more intense, was upon them and lasted for a further terrible twenty-five seconds. All over the city electric lights, turned on as people leapt terrified from their beds, abruptly went out. There was a sudden uplift, a mighty wrench and twist; crash followed crash as masses of bricks fell into the streets. The dead impact of enormous weights, the splintering of wood and the crumbling of masonry were the savage accompaniments of the dreadful dancing skyline.

Very few people actually saw the outside effects

of the earthquake at the moment of its occurrence because of the earliness of the hour. If it had happened in the middle of the day, not only would there have been more observers, but the human casualties must have been infinitely higher.

Even as it was, there was at least one man who claimed that he had seen the whole dreadful horror and who had the capacity to describe the terrible scene. Barrett, one of the editors of the *Examiner,* with some companions, was just leaving the offices of the newspaper after completing preparations for the morning editions. Day had dawned and the men stood together on a corner waiting for the first of the streetcars. In the almost noiseless city they were laughing at a funny story told by one of them. Suddenly the laughter died upon their lips. Barrett, a newspaperman trained to observe closely and accurately, remembered details which shock expunged from the minds of others. He and his colleagues, he said, found themselves all at once staggering and reeling. It was as though the earth were slipping quietly from under their feet. Then came a sickening sway that threw them flat on their faces, and they found it impossible to get up again onto their feet. Amazed, they saw tall buildings in a crazy dance. Then it seemed that their heads must split with the roar of sound. Big buildings were crumbling —clouds of dust flew up with flying timbers; wild high jangles of glass were the overtures to the crash of

75

storms of masonry. Straight ahead of them a great cornice crushed a man as if he were a maggot. Everywhere people were on all fours, like crawling bugs. Trolley tracks were twisted, their wires down, wriggling like snakes and sparking blue sparks. The streets were gashed with wounds; from some water was flooding while from others came a deadly odor of gas. The journalists, almost alone together in the nightmare scene, felt that the end of the world had come.

The fabulous Palace Hotel on Market Street had its luxurious bedrooms crammed with distinguished people. One of its original features, the covered courtyard, had been abolished with the coming of the automobile and had become a dining room largely used by the wealthy inhabitants of San Francisco. Splendid parties were held there, and the food then, as now, was famous.

On the night of the earthquake many members of the Metropolitan Opera Company, including Caruso himself, were staying at the Palace. At the actual time of the tremblor most people were asleep after the delights and exertions of the preceding evening, but, once it had happened, the commotion inside the hotel was near to panic. Caruso himself, instead of snatching up his clothes and valuables, threw open his window and, just to see that his voice was unaffected, let out what he afterwards said were the grandest notes he ever hit in his life. After that impromptu performance, he hurried downstairs and sat upon his valise in the middle of the street—a rather comic figure quite unregarded in the general commotion.

Another guest at the Palace had $600 in gold under his pillow. The shock threw him violently out of bed, whereupon he grabbed his clothes (and presumably his gold) and rushed down as fast as he could in the darkness: all the lights had gone, and the pale light of dawn hardly penetrated the gloom. People seemed to be crushed to death on all sides of him, buildings swayed, streets cracked, and chasms extended in all directions. In the extraordinary excitement he thought he saw a whole drove of cattle drop into one wide fissure. It was the sort of fantastic tale that stirred the imagination of everyone who heard it.

But not everyone panicked in the Palace Hotel like the singer or the man with the gold. Guy Giffen, a young man who was also sleeping there that night, was not unduly alarmed. He was accustomed to earthquakes, and though the shock seemed to be particularly severe, he was not frightened. But he did feel that it would be best to dress quickly and to leave his rocking bedroom if only to see what was happening and what he could do to help.

Outside in Market Street all was confusion and fear. For ordinary people whose small homes had suddenly become deathtraps there was nowhere to go but out into the open as quickly as possible. In the crowd was a young girl without husband or family. She was about to have a baby and the first labor pains were upon her. Hospital seemed far away, and the whole world was collapsing about her. Giffen, an observant young man, saw her almost at once as he emerged from his hotel. Her face was dark with pain and she had hurriedly taken refuge under an archway where she sank down, prepared to wait like an animal for her child to be born. Giffen had spent much of his time in and around medical schools and hospitals, and thought he had better see if he could help her. He happened to have a piece of string in his pocket and, oddly enough, an old spoon. With these as his only instruments he safely delivered the young mother of the baby-that-couldn't-wait. Having seen to her comfort as best he could, the self-appointed midwife took on the job of delivering babies as his work for that terrible day, and in the course of it he actually helped four more children into the world.

Not everyone was wealthy in San Francisco, and there were many who could never enter the famous hotels or possess a house of their own. For them it was a question of cheap lodging houses always crammed to capacity and never free of the smell of dirt and stale, badly cooked food. On the morning of the earthquake a lodger in one of them awoke feeling that he and the whole teeming house in which he lived were being carried bodily along on the waves of the Pacific. He was not at once alarmed. Though nights at the opera were not for him, there were plenty of other places in which to have a night out in San Francisco; and he had crawled back into his verminous bed in the early hours of the morning hardly aware of what he was doing. What more natural than that he should have a hangover?

Wishing to steady himself, he fixed his aching eyes on a particular patch of dirt on the ceiling hoping in that way to find some kind of stability. Suddenly there was an appalling crash; the odds and ends of furniture about the room came hurtling down on his bed and the very spot on the ceiling that he had hoped to subdue into some sort of immobility cracked apart. Shocked into full consciousness and realizing that after all this was something more than a drunken dream, he saw a small, bare child's foot appear through the crack. For a moment it dangled helplessly there like some ghastly hanging lamp, then the room swayed back again into an approximately vertical position, the crack in the ceiling closed up, and the tiny foot, snapped off at the ankle, fell down soft and bleeding onto his bed. The horror of it combined with the continued shaking of the house scared the man into violent action. He leapt from his frowsty bed, jumped clean through the window, landed on a side street, and lay still. He was not dead,

79

but shock and his desperate jump left him too scared to move. As soon as the dust had cleared, rescuers scrambled over the great heap that had once been a lodging house, prodding with their feet and tearing with their hands at the debris and calling all the time, "Hey, is there anyone in there?" Their cries were met with silence. If anyone was buried there it seemed that they were dead.

It was impossible to build up a composite picture from the broken mosaics of a thousand such incidents. Everywhere people were emerging into the streets clad in their night clothes. They were dazed by the sudden awakening from sleep into a terror they could not immediately understand. Most of them knew about earthquakes, but nothing on that scale had ever happened before. It seemed that the whole city was about to collapse, that their world was ruined. The front walls of shops had fallen out into the street leaving their contents exposed to view as in some of the giant dolls' houses of the day, where the whole street wall was a hinged door that could be flung open for children to play with its interior. China, often flung to the ground, candy, joints of meat, furniture and fabrics—all were freely exposed within touching distance of the crowds on the street.

In a short time everyone was foraging desperately for food. Their own stocks at home had had to be abandoned, and they sensed that there would soon be a shortage in the nightmare town. Bread,

above all, was rapidly seized from the bakers'
shops, and the desperate game went on all over the
stricken area until the authorities commandeered
all food and began to bring some order into the
chaos.

Among the thousands who had been so roughly
jolted out of sleep was Eleanor Ketchum—Mrs.
Paul N. Snyder, as she subsequently became. The
child was roughly awakened by a sound like the
crashing of the world. Instinctively she threw the
covers of her bed over her face to protect it, but almost at once she was completely buried by a weight
of falling plaster. The entire ceiling of her bedroom,
which was at the top of the house, had fallen down
on top of her, and when at length she managed
to struggle free she could see the pale light of the
dawn sky above her instead of the pretty patterned
paper to which she had been accustomed. Before
she had time for the terror to seize hold of her the
door of her bedroom was violently forced open
and her brother-in-law, in whose house she was
staying, shouted to ask if she was all right. There
were two bedrooms on the top story; Eleanor slept
in one and Anna the maid in the other. Eleanor,
determined not to be left alone in the chaos of her
ruined room, climbed over the debris and went with
her brother-in-law along the passage to Anna's
room which was separated from hers by a chimney.
The two of them hardly noticed the piles of plaster

81

in the passage, so intent were they on their purpose. They managed to force open the door of Anna's room. But Anna was dead. The high chimney had collapsed and smashed down through the roof on top of the sleeping girl, who had been killed instantaneously.

The whole back of the house was open to the sky, and, as nothing could be done for Anna, Eleanor and her companion went downstairs, their one idea being to get clear of the doomed house. On the front porch they found Eleanor's sister standing with her baby in her arms and shouting "Help, Help!" in a curious small voice paralyzed by fear. Indeed it seemed impossible to shout in that dreadful moment, for the silence in the dazed city was oppressive after the terrible noise of the tremblor. The house was in Sacramento Street where the cables of the streetcars had been broken and there was a horrible quiet. People seemed to be wandering about in a daze saying nothing—Eleanor had never "heard" such an impressive silence; the horror of it remained with her all her life. Since there was no fresh milk for the baby the family decided to try to leave the city, although, since the banks were closed, they only had the money that was in the house. However, they were fortunate enough to have a car with a tank full of gasoline and in this they drove by a circuitous route to the Ferry Building. Eleanor looked back as they drove slowly along and saw the unfinished Fairmont Hotel, on top of

Nob Hill, ablaze from every window. After crossing the Bay by ferry they drove to a friend's house in Alameda. There, while passing through the streets, they saw women in pretty dresses sitting quietly under the trees with their friends and drinking cool drinks—a most striking contrast to the sufferings, distress, and death a few short miles away in San Francisco.

Children who lived through the earthquake hardly seemed to think it frightening or terrible. Their young minds had no experience of disaster or pain, nor, on the other hand, were they old enough to think of the earth as their friend. They had built nothing as yet upon the apparently solid surface of the world; they were uncommitted. They lived in the moment, as all children do, and as they did not at all realize what the Disaster meant in terms of human ruin they were not, like their elders, terrified lest the enemy should strike again.

There was, for example, the story of the little boy. His father was a short man and not very strong, but his grandfather, who lived with them, was over six feet tall and seemed like a giant to the child. As the quake increased in force and fury the boy ran not to his puny father but to the older, stronger grandfather who had so often told stories of past earthquakes, crying: "Come and get the bad man, he's shaking the house down."

Other children found it immensely comic to see a
man on the street wearing three hats, one on top of
the other, because he wanted to save them all. Yet
others even found the refugees funny—again they
had no experience, and no idea of what the sight
really meant. But to see a man dragging a trunk-
ful of precious possessions bumpety-bump along the
street, with the load fastened to his waist with
straps as though he were a horse, was amusing,
not tragic, to their young minds. And of course it
was fun to see fully stocked shops open to the streets
because their outside wall had fallen down. It was
only much later, as they got tired, that the children
began to beg to go home, too often to be sadly answered, "Honey, we haven't a home. We have to
stay right here."

Young George Thompson lived with his parents in
the Mission District where the situation at times
was desperate. His only thought immediately after
the quake was to save the new uniforms which his
class in high school had just been issued, for he was
very proud of them. Despite the tremendous noise,
which he confessed had been frightening, he and his
brother succeeded with a friend in removing the
precious uniforms to their school where, along with
the school, they were destroyed next day. After completing their dedicated task George and his brother
sneaked back home again to see what had happened there. They found that their parents had been

ordered out by the police and had left for the hills with directions that the boys should follow them. But they had other ideas. They waited until the policeman's back was turned and then climbed quickly into their home, which was still unharmed. They were longing to see all they could, so they drew their beds up to the window and prepared to watch the "fun." But they were tired children and were soon fast asleep. Providence must have watched over them in the Mission District that night, for they survived unharmed. George lived on to found the Bear Photo Company, and he collected all the finest pictures of the Great Disaster that he had, on the whole, enjoyed.

Young Leonora Chase found her experiences fascinating. She was a girl with an eye for picture stories, and she greatly enjoyed the spices and flavors of her adventures without at all understanding the tragedy behind them. The sight of the world rocking outside her window when she awoke struck her as very comic, and the comedy was enhanced when her father, who struggled into her room to bring her out, could only stand upright by holding tightly onto the doorpost, staggering about in a drunken way most uncharacteristic of the medical profession to which he belonged.

When the order was given that no one was to cook inside their house, Leonora was highly amused at the sight of all the neighbors cooking in improvised fireplaces in the street. She did not in the least realize the terror in the minds of her elders lest the repeated shocks of that nightmare day would cause not only the hastily built fireplaces but, far more important, the precious houses still standing behind them to collapse in ruin. She did not yet understand that earth had become the enemy. Her child's shrewdness, however, soon saw that some of the grown-up men who were busy building the cooking places were much more ingenious than others. Some, utilizing all the fallen bricks they could find, made a workmanlike job of it, while others, less inventive, could only manage the very minimum which their wives could manage to cook on. Some, too, quickly surrounded their part of the pavement with blankets and screens for privacy while others, perhaps more badly scared, just carried on in the open. Not that any of them were private from Leonora. The little girl spent most of that first day joyously running up and down the street and reporting to her mother just what good smells were coming from the neighbors' "kitchens" and what everyone was having for dinner. One further thing amused her all her life in recollection. When the Chases' store of canned foods had given out, and food-distributing centers had been formed, her mother was only too thankful to avail herself of them. She sent Leonora along with a particularly fastidious and well-dressed aunt (no doubt she had put on all her newest clothes to make sure of saving them) to get what supplies the family might be entitled to. Arrived at the line, the two of them were briskly told to hold up their skirts and carry home the food they were given in the "bags" thus improvised. The stylish aunt was horrified. Her new tailor-made ran serious risk of being spoiled by the rice, eggs, butter and bread which were incontinently thrown into her lifted skirt!

To Ethel McAllister, a girl of sixteen, it seemed as though the end of the world had come when she wakened up to see a large painting in her bedroom swaying to and fro before her astonished eyes. Not that the end of the world meant a great deal—it was just a phrase she remembered from a book full of excitingly lurid pictures. She was simply fascinated by the extraordinary movement in her well-known bedroom. The picture in motion was the most interesting sight she had ever seen, and in addition she could not fail to notice that a peculiar noise, a sort of muffled roar, was coming up at her through the house. Suddenly there was a loud crash and Ethel sat up in bed. What in the world was that? She jumped out of bed and ran over to open the door. But, unexpectedly, the familiar operation was not so easy. There were bookcases in the passage outside her room and they had toppled over, spilling their heavy contents and partly jamming her bedroom door. All the same, she managed to squeeze through and, after nimbly climbing over a mountain of slipping books, ran downstairs to join the family.

By that time things were really exciting, and what the family then did was typical of what San Franciscans in their thousands were beginning to do all over the wrecked area. As the first shock wore off, everyone wanted to see how the city had suffered, and when Mr. Shields, a kind, rich neighbor, called in his new automobile to ask if any of the family would like to take a drive to see what had happened in the city below, Ethel, true to the brave tradition of the McAllisters, at once said she would like to go. A ride in an automobile those days was not to be missed, for there were very few of them about, and it was with surprise that people found that they rescued more people than they killed. Her mother said that she might as well see if she could rescue Great-aunt Martha from the Hotel Bella Vista on Van Ness. Ethel had always been morbidly fascinated by the old lady, a self-made invalid who lived in semidarkness and a hushed atmosphere, and she thought it would be fun to try to get her out into the exciting daylight. So she set out, and Mr. Shields made Van Ness his first call. Of course the old lady refused to budge (later she was compelled by the police to walk away instead of being comfortably driven), but Ethel, young though she was, stopped at the Bella Vista long enough to collect one suitcase full of valuable silver and an-

other of clothes before driving on down to Market
Street to see what there was to be seen.

At the same time, though she did not know it, her
brother set out to rescue their uncle, dumb and semi-
paralyzed, from where he lived in a dangerous
part of the town. As they had no wheel chair,
Tony McAllister took with him a small armchair
on casters, and when he found his uncle he put
him in the chair and pushed him painfully uphill
for some miles to a hospital in a safer quarter.
Afterward, when the family tried to trace the invalid again, they found he had been moved, and
since he could not speak and had nothing on him in
the way of identification, he could not be traced. It
took three months and every kind of advertisement
and other means before he was discovered in a
hospital in an outlying part of the city.

By this time the whole frightful scene was being
observed with a professional eye. Arnold Genthe,
a young and very good-looking photographer, was
the rage in San Francisco. Everyone wanted him
to photograph them, for his approach to art was
radically different from anything seen before. He
deliberately took pictures out of focus, lighted his
subjects from the rear, and, from being poor and
unknown, he had rapidly risen to be one of the most
famous and lionized people in the city. On the evening before the Disaster he had had a pleasant
supper party with friends followed by a delightful

evening at the opera. But not long after he got to bed he was awakened by the crashing of his collection of valuable Chinese porcelain (he never again collected—his interest seemed to have been killed on that dreadful morning). His Japanese servant, even more accustomed to earthquakes than the San Franciscan, came in to say that he was leaving at once to collect all the food he could find. He never returned to Genthe, but his master afterward saw him with a large parcel of eatables strapped across his back. Left alone in his apartment, Genthe dressed himself, for some unexplained reason in his riding clothes, which he was to wear for several weeks. He then went out and tried to make his way to the St. Francis Hotel, where he had friends. En route, being an observant man, he noted a strange little drama. The front of a third-floor bedroom at Delmonico's had fallen into the street carrying with it a chair that had some clothes piled upon it. The owner, standing precariously in his nightwear on the edge of the precipice, called down to a passing workman: "Do you want to make twenty dollars?"

"Sure," replied the man. "What is it?"

"See that suit there? I want you to bring it up to me here."

But just as the fellow was preparing to earn his money another shock came and made him think better of it.

"Ah, you'd better come and get it yourself," he yelled above the din to the frightened and frustrated owner above.

Genthe found a cheerful spirit at the St. Francis. When he offered payment for what he had eaten, the waiter refused the money saying, "No charge today, sir, as long as things hold out." Whatever the hotel had was gladly shared on that disastrous morning.

By that time the great Caruso had found his way over to the St. Francis from the abandoned Palace Hotel. Waiters hovered about the important guest as though trying to make up for the way their city had betrayed him. Caruso was alone and not disposed to be talkative. His week's engagement was at an end after only one performance, and he himself had been seriously frightened. Genthe observed that he was smoking a cigarette and muttering to himself over and over again words which sounded like " 'Ell of a place, 'ell of a place. I never come back." And he never did. He took the first available train out of San Francisco and six days later was back in New York. To friends there who asked him about his experiences in the Disaster he replied shortly, "Give me Vesuvius."

Genthe and his friends sat talking and drinking wine in the St. Francis as long as they could. Genthe gave them a toast, repeating the famous words from Horace: "And if the whole world collapse he will stand fearless among the falling ruins." The future of their beautiful city seemed terrifyingly uncertain, but Genthe, the artist photographer, felt a compulsion to be out in the streets, to see and to suffer with the rest. And when at last he went, the world was rocking around him. Afterward he said that the scene in San Francisco that morning reminded him of the largest, grandest Cecil B. DeMille film that even that inspired director—the sensation of the post-Disaster years—could ever have imagined. But DeMille was not directing, said Genthe; that day the Lord Himself had taken charge.

All day and for many days the photographer wandered from end to end of the city, capturing with his camera the physical aspect of its agony as well as the strained and anxious faces of his fellow citizens. When at last he returned to his abandoned studio he found the place wrecked and his thousands of photographic plates reduced to chunks of useless, fantastically shaped glass.

What happened in San Francisco that sunny April morning? The earth, on and from which fortune had come, rose and struck the city a mighty swinging blow. The danger which everyone had ignored crashed down upon it. San Francisco was in the grip of the greatest earthquake ever recorded.

The San Andreas fault had moved or crept northward relative to the continental side. Its creeping caused violent rotary motion in places within a radius of fifty miles; but the great city had to bear by far the most terrible damage.

It had always been known that shoddy building materials had been used in San Francisco, and poor brickwork—often a mere veneer—was the cause of much of the damage. Time after time buildings constructed in that way disintegrated completely during the tremblor. On the other hand, buildings like St. Dominic's Church, massive in design and honestly constructed, did not disintegrate but instead tended to fall apart in enormous pieces, complete with masonry, many tons in weight. Ironically these "honest pieces" were, of course, a great danger to the crowds that filled the streets seeking to escape danger in their own homes. The massive fragments from buildings like the church hung and crashed together, cutting completely through sidewalks as they fell and sweeping everything and everybody from their path.

On the whole, steel-framed buildings stood up well against the earth's attack. They were not destroyed in spite of their alarming rhythmical swing which made onlookers watch them in terrified amazement until, with the end of the quake, they slowly grew still again. At one time even the famous, spectacular *Call* building was observed to be hanging out of vertical plumb by more than a foot, that same building where in the very early hours all those newsy headlines had been gaily set up for the city's cosmopolitan population.

The oscillation of some buildings produced extraordinary results. In one case some bricks from a falling chimney hit the ground not immediately below, but as much as forty-five or fifty feet away. In another a house was seen to jump four feet off its foundation and then bump for a fleeting second along the ground. In that house lived a lonely lady who survived the experience but who felt, she said, "like corn in a popper." In yet another case a man's front yard seemed to him to have shifted sixteen feet. That might well have been an exaggeration, though its fundamental truth and that of the other stories of earthquake freaks explained only too clearly the terrible feeling that morning that the city was in the grip of some supernatural horror. Stories of dead and dying flew across the city from mouth to mouth. There again, there was much exaggeration, but there was enough truth in the rumors to cause terror; as, for instance, when seventy-five bodies were taken from a three-floored lodging house at Fifth and Minna Streets and when one hundred and fifty hapless people were reported dead at the Brunswick Hotel at Seventh and Mission Streets.

Steel framing badly encased in masonry was savagely tested, and the destruction of the fine-looking City Hall of which San Franciscans were so proud was felt to be a public disgrace. This building—similar in design to the one that stands today—was in classical style with a splendid dome supported on three tiers of pillars. It appeared to be so strong and solid that nothing in the world could ever destroy it, but the earthquake of 1906 found out its weakness. The pillars of the monster seven-million-dollar building proved to be neither solid nor honestly built, and when the frame began to rock, the masonry that clothed them simply fell off into the street leaving nothing but the pathetic skeleton surmounted by the still-solid dome as a monument to the folly of man and the strength of natural disasters. The earthquake had uncovered its strange secret, and the ruins cried to heaven the shame of the men who built it.

At 5.13 that morning there were few about who could see its fearful downfall. But at least one spectator was actually within a stone's throw. He saw the ground rising and falling with a most extraordinary motion like the ocean at ebb tide. Then came the crash. Tons upon tons of the mighty pile slid away from the steel framework with a noise like thunder. "Keep to the middle of the road," he shouted to one of his friends, for it was impossible to judge what the length of that shock might be. He himself was thrown upon his back onto the pulsating pavement. All around him huge buildings danced, wobbled, and veered. Then came a lull.

95

But the most appalling shock was yet to come. The street heaved again more terrifyingly than ever. The old Supreme Court danced a frivolous frolic. Houses resumed their fantastic, ogreish dancing. One long line of frame buildings tottered and then, as a score or more of white-shirted humanity made a wild dash for the open, it was laid flat.

The Valencia Street Hotel—one of San Francisco's older buildings—was frame-built on made-up ground, and on the morning of the disaster it was full of guests. At the moment of the earthquake a huge mass of asphalt on which its foundations rested collapsed. The whole of the famous old building, complete with its inhabitants, toppled and sagged forward with appalling speed and finality. Rescue teams did their best, but the Valencia was the burial place of more than forty people.

At the same moment that the old Valencia Street Hotel slumped over, a whole row of frame houses on 18th Street was twisted completely around by the shock of the earthquake. As ever, rescuers were soon on the scene, for bands of helpers were never far away on that terrible morning. Amid the usual piles of debris, the loose stones and the cracked ground they found the dead body of a man. And he was not alone; in his arms, clasped tightly for safety, was a safe and smiling baby. As the men gently took her from that tragic embrace they looked for her mother, but she was nowhere to be found.

Suddenly the end of the tremblor came, as abruptly as it had begun. Ruin endeavored to outdo ruin; a world of structural work found refuge on the fickle earth amid deep clouds of dust. The man who had seen it all made his way home through a world where, he said, everyone seemed temporarily insane. There was terror in their faces but their voices showed that mysterious enjoyment which maniacs sometimes have in killing and gloating over their prey.

It was hard to imagine that beautiful San Francisco, so modern and apparently so strong, could actually be moved bodily even a few inches. Yet that was exactly what happened more or less throughout the city, and afterward large sums of money had to be spent in pulling houses back into the straight again. More spectacular, but less expensive to put right, were the streetcar tracks, some of which in Market Street itself hung suspended ten feet in the air. The extraordinary rippling of the ground had certain beauty, but it showed clearly that earth had taken on the attributes of its sister element, the ever-moving water. "Oh sir," exclaimed a night watchman describing his experiences, "the ground in Franklin Street rolled just like the waves of the sea."

As the first dead began to come by, a touch of the macabre was added to a scene of crazy destruction. Corpses were piled high in a hastily commandeered automobile like carcasses in a butcher's wagon—all bloody with crushed skulls, broken limbs, and crushed faces. At first those who saw the horrid sight were filled with fear; for a moment the quake seemed to have subsided, but who knew when a fresh one might begin, and who knew where the next victims might be found? The familiar world was gone and nothing was safe. It was already known that a score or more people had been drowned in the ill-fated Mission District, and to the fevered imagination of those whose eyes had been appalled by the shocking sights it seemed as though the loss of life might be enormous. The crowds in the streets seemed unnaturally quiet; even the children did not cry. The fear of God was upon them all. No one knew what might happen next.

However, San Franciscans were notoriously of a cheerful, brave, and optimistic disposition. It was not long after the subsidiary quakes, which to everyone's immense relief were mild and harmless, that friends and neighbors, persuading themselves that all danger was past, began making up parties to tour the sights just as Mr. Shields and his party had. Disaster had come and gone; there was, certainly, a good deal of damage, but San Francisco was a rich city and all that would soon be put right. The most important thing was that the vast majority of people were safe and that the terrible noise which had appalled human imagi-

98

nation had stopped at last. It might have been a great deal worse.

All over the city people began talking and laughing again. Strangers exchanged anecdotes freely with anyone they happened to meet in the street, even if they were dressed in the oddest fashion—very likely in their night clothes. Everyone was vastly relieved. True, there were a few puffs of smoke to be seen in the bright blue sky, but that was only to be expected—the city had had fires before. Yet there was certainly no cause for fear in that respect, for San Francisco had prudently built up what was said to be the finest fire-fighting force on the entire continent of America. Their firemen, citizens were confident, would soon put an end to such small outbreaks as might occur.

There was a good deal for the tourist parties to look at after the earthquake. The earth-enemy had certainly done his work well. In places familiar streets had sunk as much as three or four feet, while in others the contrary had occurred and great humps had suddenly appeared. A confused mass of electric wires in weird and incongruous shapes lay about in all directions, some still sparking the blue sparks which Mr. Barrett had observed at the outset. Wagons with horses still hitched to them, horses and drivers all dead, lay about on the streets where they had been struck down by the mass of fallen bricks. In one part of the city money, its chief preoccupation, was spilled on the ground. But it was useless money, for the bills (some 5,000 dollars' worth) were torn, halved and quartered, destroyed no doubt by someone crazed with fear and certain of losing everything anyway.

Men who had gone to bed wealthy now thought themselves penniless. There seemed little difference between them and the lunatic who had torn up his money or the poor old chap who, too tired to go farther, sat down on a garbage can and waited for the giant *Call* building to fall on him. "What's the use," he asked, "what's the use? I'm old and tired and I haven't any money. What's the use?"

Pavements were still pulsating as the tourists began their excited round and voices were pitched high to make themselves heard above the din of the resurrected city. There were clouds of dust everywhere and everyone was a little insane. Some people were no doubt still frightened, for small shocks continued to shake the earth, but many laughed loud and long at the feeblest jokes and all felt themselves united by their great deliverance. One gaudy lady who might have come from the Barbary Coast itself was heard to shout above the tumult that as long as her money lasted she would certainly have a good time. She did not know how long she would have to wait before she could enjoy herself.

FIVE

DOWN at Palo Alto on the San Francisco Peninsula the Leland Stanford University, which lay close to the San Andreas fault, suffered severely from the earthquake in common with many other places in the Bay area.

Happily for her, Mrs. Stanford, the university's great benefactress, had died two years earlier. Her chief concern had been that the campus, built in the romanesque style and of a soft yellow stone that would have looked perfectly in place in Spain, should have the finest architects and sculptors that could be found. She searched Europe to find the men she wanted, and when she had found them set them to work regardless of expense. It would certainly have broken her heart when the spire of the fine Memorial Chapel fell into the chancel, covering everything with debris, so that only the heads of Italian marble statues of the twelve apostles emerged from the mess.

Indeed the whole campus looked like a battle ground when the quake was over. Many handsome buildings, including the library, one of the dormitories, and the gymnasium, were demolished, and the debris was flung far and wide.

Paul Edwards, a freshman, was of course in bed at the time of the shock. Although very young, he was already interested in journalism and, together with a friend, he had got himself appointed correspondent of a San Francisco paper—in his case the *Daily News*. It has always been said that the feeling of an earthquake shock cannot, any more than its noise, be properly described, though once experienced it is never forgotten. Edwards knew immediately that this might be one of the great moments of his life and he was up and dressed in a twinkling. He made a round of the campus, noting the severity of the damage and listening to the comments of his seniors on all that had occurred to wreck Mrs. Stanford's loving and costly work. It seemed to Edwards that this domestic disaster was just about as bad as it could be, and he hastily consulted with his journalist friend. At that time no one had any idea of what was happening in San Francisco and both boys agreed that it was clearly their duty (and very possibly their pleasure) to report to their papers at the earliest possible moment. It was a long haul into town from Palo Alto, so they decided to hire horses and a rig from a livery stable in order to get there quicker and also to save their legs.

It was a clear, shining morning of blue skies and the air was scented with roses as they set out on the road between the flat Bay Shore and what is nowadays the Skyline Boulevard. They passed the ridges of hills cleft by the long lakes of the San Andreas fault (of whose share in the disaster they had at that time no notion) and covered the twenty-four-odd miles to Colma with little difficulty. There, however, to their amazement, they were informed that if they carried out their plan of driving on into the city their horses would certainly be commandeered by the soldiers in charge of San Francisco. This was the young journalists' first inkling of the great tragedy that lay ahead of them; but, being prudent boys, they at once decided to stable their horses and lay up their rig to make quite sure that they would not be charged with their loss should they be taken from them. From Colma on— a distance of well over ten miles—their duty as journalists would compel them to walk.

When they came to the top of the Potrero ridge they were astounded and even a little frightened by the stark horror of the scene that met their eyes. Instead of the sweet scent of roses the acrid smell of stifling smoke lay on the air. The sun had vanished in the murk, and below them San Francisco was an inferno of smoke and flame. It was even difficult to make out any of the familiar landmarks in the city; perhaps they had disappeared; who could tell what horror awaited the two young men in the stricken town? But the young are not easily deterred, and besides, Paul Edwards and his friend were journalists. If Stanford and its damage were news, San Francisco was infinitely more exciting.

They plunged down into the city and walked on and on, right into its burning heart where the very stones around them seemed to be glowing incandescent. And there their walk came to an abrupt end. They were stopped by the military, who refused to allow them to go farther. Both boys protested that they were pressmen and should be allowed to pass, but the soldiers were adamant and even mocking, to the young men's great chagrin. "You sit down right there and take it easy," they said. "Your offices burned out hours ago." The friends had no alternative but to obey, though they subsequently found that in the case of Edwards the information was inaccurate. The *News* office was not in the center of the town but a little farther out, and with the help of a hand-operated job press (since there was no electric power) the staff managed to produce the only newspaper issued in the city on that first terrible day of the Disaster. Unfortunately they had to do it without the help of young Edwards from Stanford.

Some of the sight-seeing parties who had started out to see the damage as soon as the earthquake shocks seemed over noticed a yellow glow on the skyline which both excited and puzzled them. The quarter down by the Mission was lit by a strange light quite different from their beloved San Francisco sun, a light that set hearts beating and caused people, lately so thankful for the end of the terrible earthquake noise and danger of destruction, to catch their breath and wonder if some new horror might not turn on them. So began, a mere half hour after the tremor, the greatest conflagration of modern times or, at the very best, the greatest in times of peace. The terrible element of fire—so fearfully familiar in San Francisco—had joined sister earth in a savage attack on the city.

But even when they saw the flames, citizens did not feel unduly worried, for the fame of their fire-fighting force gave them a feeling of security. There could hardly be much danger of a conflagration on the old pattern with such experienced men in command. The gallant crews would, they felt sure, soon have the fire under control. So there was no rush home to save valuable property. The early-morning terror had brought on a dangerous inertia; to most people it was extremely distasteful to go back into houses newly shaken which might still be potential traps. Every few minutes there had been light aftershocks; who could say if there might not yet be another and even worse shake than the mighty tremblor of the early hours? Better risk a small fire which would surely be quickly put out than another earthquake in houses which offered them no possible security. So it was that in the city's most dangerous hour many people were about the streets while others had one idea only—to make coffee and cook breakfast. Both occupations, as it happened, added to the general peril.

When the time of supreme trial came the fire crews were without their leader. Sullivan, perhaps the greatest fire chief they had ever known, and the idol of a city that had nevertheless refused to listen to his warnings, was dead. He had been killed, together with his wife, by a falling chimney in the terrible moment of the earthquake, and when the call, so long awaited, came he could not answer. His deputy, Dougherty, a brave and experienced man, took charge, but he was not the leader that Sullivan had been.

On that morning Rudi Schubert had been in the

Fire Force just nine months. He was coming off duty when the earthquake shook the town so alarmingly and he at once reported back to headquarters on Taylor Street. There he found that the side walls of the brick Fire House had been badly cracked—twelve inches at the top and narrowing downward. In a short time other men began to turn up, for they knew that with a quake of such force there was bound to be fire and they had to be ready for trouble. No fire alarm ever came through owing to the fact that the alarm system depended on electrical current generated by tiers of batteries which had all been toppled over and destroyed by the earthquake.

Earth had done its work well, and now fire started with an immense advantage, for the general conflagration in San Francisco began without the city's Fire Force being officially alerted.

Fifty-two fires were individually reported and thirty-eight horse-drawn fire engines existed. Two-thirds of the fires were small—most of them due to cracked brick flues and the use of coal for heating post-earthquake coffee and cooking breakfast. A notable example of the small fire with consequences out of all proportion to its size was the famous "ham and eggs" fire, caused by a housewife who lived on the far side of Van Ness Avenue, a long way away from any other outbreak. Unaware that she had a broken gas main she put on a good breakfast of ham and eggs to cook for her family, and her well-intentioned act caused a fire that swept through Hayes Valley, leveling a score of city blocks and causing the only extensive damage west of Van Ness.

Under normal conditions, with a proper alarm system and plenty of water, most of the early fires would have been under control by noon, but this was not to be.

As smoke had already been seen even though there were no alarms, Schubert's company set out immediately to look for its own fires. All over the city the rest of the thirty-eight companies were fire-hunting too, and the very fact of their wide dispersal brought its own dangers, for it was partly lack of co-ordination that allowed the fire to take such a terrible stranglehold on the city.

When Schubert first set out it was still quite easy to get through the streets. Most of the debris was lying on the sidewalks, where brick veneer had fallen away from wooden buildings which had outwardly seemed solidly brick-built. To add to the general weakness of structure in buildings, the bricks themselves were in the main bound with lime mortar, not with cement. Everything was thus much looser and fell to pieces far more easily. Schubert, in those early stages of the fire, found only two streets impassable; no one could get by the ruined City Hall, and the road by the Post Office was blocked by immense heaps of rubble which, in the event, were not moved for three days. His company went to work on its first fire in Market Street cheerfully enough. They were well-trained, confident men, and they never doubted their ability to put it out. Hoses were coupled up to the nearest hydrant, ready to work at ninety pounds to the square inch pressure—the same pressure as firemen start with today. When the hydrant was turned on, instead of a strong, steady flow only a thin trickle of water came through, then mud, then nothing. Schubert and his friends thought the hydrant must be defective and tried another, and then yet another. The same thing happened each time. There was no water; the supply had failed.

The failure would not have surprised Fire Chief Sullivan had he lived to see it. He had warned the city over and over again that as the whole water supply came in at a point that crossed the San Andreas fault (which, as was well known, might creep at any time) it was thoroughly unsafe. The events of April 18th showed that his warning was fully justified. At the moment of the earthquake the 30-inch mains cracked in at least three places at the spot where they crossed the fault, with the inevitable result that the entire water supply for San Francisco was abruptly cut off. Service pipes leading to private houses from the scattered storage cisterns were also cracked and the cisterns quickly drained dry.

So it happened that the great element of water,

sister to earth and fire, was tearing headlong away from the city, in her moment of extreme danger, down to the ocean all around in which was contained three-fifths of all the water of the world. But there were no appliances for pumping salt water, and San Francisco had to do without.

In their utter frustration the firemen remembered a large water tank on the Hopkins estate at the top of Nob Hill, and as it was independent of the main supply this was serviceable for a time. But soon that water too was all gone—it was but a drop in the total amount needed that day—and the men were again powerless while all over San Francisco fires were increasing rapidly. By midday the fire was officially declared to be a conflagration, that is, it was completely out of control, and the whole of the city east of Van Ness Avenue seemed to be ablaze.

The plight of the town was now extremely serious, and people who saw the empty hoses uselessly trailing from hydrants and cisterns knew the true meaning of fear. Bands of firemen all over the city looked at one another in horror. Without water they were impotent. The military moved in and suggested dynamite. The only way to prevent the whole city from burning, they said, was to blow up certain key properties that lay in the van of the fire and so stop it short at that point—the old nineteenth-century method.

The first dynamiting was not an unqualified success. Too much dynamite was used, and in the wrong places, so that flimsily built houses were blown apart instead of being simply collapsed. In this way interior woodwork was bared and exposed to the enormous heat of adjoining fires with the result that it kindled before any flames reached it. In general the plan was that soldiers cleared out the houses as the dynamiting squads advanced, but in one lodging house near the Embarcadero, Schubert, himself one of the dynamiters, found a number of men lying unconscious, either drunk or drugged—either was common enough in San Francisco. The fireman dragged at the heavy, prostrate forms lying on the sleazy beds, but two could not be moved and had to be left to be blown up with the house.

The dynamiting of property in San Francisco that day reminded his firemen that their great and much-loved chief, Sullivan, had long ago had some such plan for use in the event (which he always thought might be perfectly possible) of the failure of the water supply. But they had never been trained in the use of explosives and inevitably many mistakes were made. Schubert's company, in common with the others, worked on and tried every possible means of staying the terrible fire. In the crackling heat they began to light backfires which, it was thought, might be of some use. These fires burned backward toward the main conflagration and the burnt ground they left created a wider and more effective firebreak than could otherwise be arranged.

San Franciscans, now at last seeing the deadly peril of their beautiful city, accepted the dynamiting with something akin to pleasure. It was a drastic but absolutely necessary expedient, and through immediate destruction something might in the long run be saved. Meanwhile a few sections of that cosmopolitan population tried to replace the vanished water by other means, but their puny efforts could do nothing to stem the fire. Italians, having plenty of wine, poured hundreds of gallons of the precious stuff upon their houses, while other men, in desperation, tried the effect of urinating upon the flames which attacked their homes.

From the general terror and desperation some heroes emerged. Fulton G. Berry, for fifty-six years a well-known figure in the city, stood sadly contemplating his $50,000 palace, as yet untouched on Van Ness Avenue. He watched the fire come tearing toward him, and when the dynamite squad arrived he did not hesitate. "Blow her to blazes, boys," he said firmly. But having given the order he turned away and walked off; even he could not bear to watch the total destruction of his prized and precious house.

MISSION STREET IN THE PATH OF THE FIRE

THE WRECKAGE OF THE THREE-STORY VALENCIA STREET HOTEL.
NEXT DAY ALL THIS WAS CONSUMED BY THE FIRE

Frame Buildings in the Butchertown Area

Earthquake Crevices in Valencia Street

After Three Days of Earthquake and Fire in the Western Addition

The Effect of the Earthquake on Wooden Houses

Homes "South of Market" Caved in by the Force of the Earthquake

Looking East from Telegraph Hill toward the Wholesale District

Market Street. Buildings Caved in by the Earthquake and Finally Destroyed by Fire

Market and O'Farrell Streets at the Height of the Fire

The Wrecked City Hall

REFUGEES IN JEFFERSON SQUARE. THE EARTHQUAKE AND FIRE DID
NOT DESTROY THEIR SPIRIT OR THEIR SENSE OF HUMOR

RELIEF TABLES IN FRONT OF THE CITY HALL. PHOTOGRAPH BY
ARNOLD GENTHE, 1906

SAN FRANCISCO IN FLAMES

SAN FRANCISCO TODAY

An anxious group of Bohemians assembled in their famous club house, each one speculating whether their premises were in danger. Most of them, however, were fairly confident that dynamite would confine the flames to the area beyond Market Street. But all too soon came the news that the Palace Hotel, the proud house that had so often withstood danger, was a raging furnace, and in a very short time—for the fire seemed to leap from place to place with demoniac speed and fury—the Bohemian block was on fire. The first thought of members was to save their works of art and, assisted by Henry the hallboy, they began tearing pictures from their frames. At that moment a truck from the Vulcan Iron Works arrived loaded with provisions and no time was lost in reloading it with pictures. But alas! The work was hardly finished when the truck was again commandeered by soldiers and all the pictures had to be carried back into the doomed club. Charles Dickson, an artist member of the Board of Directors, declared that he had done his best and that now the military had undone it all. There was a good deal of recrimination about the lack of earlier action, but at least Dickson managed to rescue from the office cards showing members' current debts for supplies! Moreover, before the building was blown up—as it was bound to be—members did manage to secure another truck onto which they were able hurriedly to load many of the club's most cherished works of art—at the eleventh hour, perhaps, but still not too late.

A famous writer was in town that dreadful day, and the Bohemian Club preserved the letter that he wrote to a friend from the safety of Glen Ellen a few days later:

DEAR MERLE,

You bet I was in the thick of it. Routed out of bed at quarter past five, half an hour later Mrs. London and I were in the saddle. We rode miles over the surrounding country. An hour after the shock, from a high place in the mountains, we could see at the same time the smoke of burning San Francisco and burning Santa Rosa. Caught a train to Santa Rosa . . . then on Wednesday afternoon we got into San Francisco and spent the whole night in the path of the flames—you bet I saw it all! Am glad all of you escaped O.K. Do I understand you are going to move to Oakland?

Affectionately
YOUR UNCLE JACK

Jack London was a very successful writer of adventurous fiction, but it may be doubted whether in his wildest imagination he had ever pictured a scene like the carpet of flame below him in burning San Francisco.

Fate had not yet finished with the agonized city. Before very long a fireman came shouting down the street that there was no more dynamite. Stocks, never very large, had been gravely depleted in the first stouthearted attempts to blow up houses. Inexperience caused the firemen to use too much of the explosive, and in many cases more harm than good had been done. In this way the precious supplies had been wasted.

There was now a continuous line of flame from north of Market Street along the waterfront to the station of the only railroad that ran out of the city. The population seemed cut off from escape, and during the first two days of the fire surprisingly few people knew of a safe but narrow way around to the Ferry Building where the boats that crossed the Bay to Berkeley and Oakland were still running. It was almost unbelievable that at such a ghastly, desperate moment, when citizens were hemmed in by a raging, roaring wall of flame, there was no panic in San Francisco.

This was partly due to extreme courage and resourcefulness in a most unlikely quarter. The fiddling, dishonest Mayor, Eugene Schmitz, was one of the heroes of the Disaster. In our own day Winston Churchill has written: "Power for the sake of lording it over our fellow creatures or adding to personal pomp is rightly judged base. But power in a national crisis, when a man believes he knows what orders should be given, is a blessing." Churchill was talking of his own power in England's moment of danger, and if the words had been written before 1906 no one would have dreamed of applying them to Mayor Schmitz. Yet in San Francisco's crisis, at the moment when her very life was in danger and when that danger might have been so terribly increased by weakness at the summit of affairs, the miracle happened and Schmitz proved himself a hero. He had the power, he believed he knew what orders should be given, and he did not hesitate to give them. He may secretly have wondered whether they would be obeyed, for he knew his enemies and he knew his record in the city. But he succeeded, and for San Francisco his power was a blessing that could hardly be overestimated.

As soon as he realized the gravity of the situation the Mayor called together a band of some fifty responsible citizens (many of whom had previously hated and despised him) and constituted them into a Relief Committee to deal with the emergency. Day after day and night after night the Committee met constantly, receiving the latest information, issuing orders and, so far as it was able, broadcasting the city's need for help to the rest of the continent. One after another its headquarters were destroyed by the fire and members had to seize such papers as they had and move on somewhere else. The situation became more and more desperate, but they worked doggedly under the Mayor's inspiring leadership, careless of personal safety and completely fearless in the face of awful danger to themselves and their city.

The Mayor's first proclamation was historic:

Let it be given out that three men have already been shot down without mercy for looting. Let it also be understood that the order had also been given to all soldiers and policemen to do likewise without hesitation in the cases of any and all miscreants who may seek to take advantage of the city's awful misfortune. I will ask the chief of police and the representatives of the Federal military authorities here present if I do not echo their sentiments in this.

Brigadier General Funston, one of the representatives referred to by the Mayor, commanded the Federal troops in the vicinity of San Francisco. He lived in the city and had seen what was happening from his beautiful home on Nob Hill. Instantly he realized the danger that might arise from terror-striken people wandering leaderless in the streets of the defenseless city. With the Mayor's concurrence he called in the army on his own initiative —an act for which he might well have been court-martialed. But Funston was a brave man who had learned long ago not to think of personal safety in an emergency. Born in Ohio and brought up in Kansas, he had been in turn a journalist, botanist, and an explorer in the Klondike. He had once attracted public attention by making a perilous expedition alone in an open canoe down the Yukon, after which he had joined the insurgent Cuban army and learned all there was to know about guerrilla fighting. Still on the lookout

117

PROCLAMATION
BY THE MAYOR

The Federal Troops, the members of the Regular Police Force and all Special Police Officers have been authorized by me to KILL any and all persons found engaged in Looting or in the Commission of Any Other Crime.

I have directed all the Gas and Electric Lighting Co.'s not to turn on Gas or Electricity until I order them to do so. You may therefore expect the city to remain in darkness for an indefinite time.

I request all citizens to remain at home from darkness until daylight every night until order is restored.

I WARN all Citizens of the danger of fire from Damaged or Destroyed Chimneys, Broken or Leaking Gas Pipes or Fixtures, or any like cause.

E. E. SCHMITZ, Mayor

Dated, April 18, 1906.

ALTVATER PRINT, MISSION AND 22D STS.

Wells Fargo Bank History Room, San Francisco

ONE OF MAYOR SCHMITZ'S FIRST PROCLAMATIONS

for adventure, he served gallantly in the Philippine wars, where he picked up the auspicious nickname of "Lucky Funston." Experienced, brave, and accustomed to command, he knew very well that in a time of real danger he must act first and ask permission afterward. It was, therefore, only natural that on April 18, 1906, he never hesitated a moment.

As all communications were long ago broken, he sent dispatch riders galloping through the streets to Fort Mason and obtained the help of 1,500 U. S. soldiers in full campaign equipment to protect San Francisco against its own lawless minority. Had he waited to consult Washington (as by army regulations he ought to have done) or searched books for a precedent for his action, he would have been too late. As it was, thanks to his brave and determined action the soldiers arrived in time, and Funston was afterward commended by the President, Theodore Roosevelt, and raised to the rank of general.

The Mayor's stern words about the shooting of looters on sight came none too soon, for it was no uncommon sight to see men trying to cut off the fingers of the dead in order to obtain their rings. Many unsuccessful attempts were made to loot food shops, but their stocks were quickly commandeered and used for the general good. Some of the looters used ingenious ruses to try to obtain the valuables they coveted. One man made a trooper believe that a dead body lying on a pile of rocks was his mother and was permitted to go up to the body. Apparently overcome by bitter grief, he threw himself down upon the corpse. But in another instant the trooper, who had his suspicions, discovered that the man was attempting to chew the earrings from the dead woman's ear. He was promptly shot, and the diamonds were found in his mouth.

It was not only the soldiers who carried out the Mayor's edict. On Stockton Street a man was caught in the very act of cutting off a dead woman's hands to obtain her locked bracelets. But he was quickly seized by the mob and strung up to a telegraph pole. Other looters, caught in the act, had placards tied around their necks which they were obliged to wear about the city. One photograph in the possession of the Society of California Pioneers shows two men displaying such placards. One stated in large letters I AM A JUNK THIEF, while his companion walked beside him with a notice around his neck proclaiming SO AM I. These were young offenders—too young to be shot, but old enough to merit a sharp lesson.

As was only natural in such a terrible situation, there were horrible sights to be seen in San Francisco that day and in the days following. Dogs, probably family pets who had been left to starve in the general excitement, devoured the bodies pulled from ruined houses, and where only a leg or an arm protruded they dug frantically to uncover the rest of the carcass. Terrible, though not without its funny side, was the plight of an Italian storekeeper, a meat dealer in the market. His nerve had gone completely, as a result of the earthquake and the fire that threatened to devour him and his possessions, and he rushed frantically into his giant refrigerator and slammed the door. There at least, he must have thought, he could not be burned. Unfortunately his absence was not noticed for several days. When the building was burned the refrigerator was unharmed, but he was not found until soldiers came much later to clear up the market. By that time the poor man was a gibbering maniac.

At the dawn of that awful day there was a single operator on duty at the San Francisco Postal Telegraph Company. At nine o'clock he sent out the following message:

THERE WAS AN EARTHQUAKE HIT US AT 5:13 THIS MORNING, WRECKING SEVERAL BUILDINGS AND OUR OFFICES. THEY ARE CARTING DEAD FROM THE FALLEN BUILDINGS. FIRE ALL OVER THE TOWN. THERE IS NO WATER, AND WE LOST OUR POWER. I'M GOING TO GET OUT OF THE OFFICE AS WE HAD A LITTLE SHAKE EVERY FEW MINUTES AND IT'S ME FOR THE SIMPLE LIFE.

While his instruments still lived he would stay by them, but afterward no one could tell what terror might be in store in the dreadful silence broken only by the roar of the flames. He could never stay in the office alone.

At 12:45 the telegraph wire was still clicking out messages on the progress of the fire. Then there was a pause. Then, desperately, a message: I'M PACKING UP THE INSTRUMENTS. Then, only a minute or two later: INSTRUMENTS ALL PACKED UP AND I'M READY TO RUN. The final message received by the outside world from the doomed city said simply, GOOD-BY.

SIX

THE great earthquake in San Francisco was recorded as far away as Birmingham in England. At first, of course, the magnitude alone was noted, and it was not known exactly where it had occurred. But, though there was only one outgoing telegraph line still working in the city, news soon trickled out all over the United States and thence to the rest of the world. The fame of San Francisco was so great, its fabulous rise to riches so well known, that the agony of its destruction was universally felt.

It was not long before messages began to pour in

from all over the American continent, and later a steady flood came from England and the continent of Europe. The Pope was particularly concerned about the victims of the Disaster and he made it his business to obtain all possible news of what was happening in San Francisco.

Naturally the agony was most deeply felt in the United States, for over and above the fact that it was an American city that was being destroyed, many people had relatives there. There was, for

EXTRA Oakland Tribune. EXTRA

VOL. LXV   OAKLAND, CALIFORNIA, THURSDAY EVENING, APRIL 19, 1906   NO. 50

CITIZENS ARE FORCED TO FIGHT FLAMES AT POINT OF REVOLVER

Three hundred thousand persons will be left homeless in San Francisco by tonight. Help is needed at once.

Wells Fargo Bank History Room, San Francisco

TOP NEWS IN THE PRESS

example, the man who had gone to New York on business leaving behind his wife and their five children. It was many days before he could discover whether his family was dead or alive. But, quite apart from personal tragedies and anxieties, there was a strong wave of national sympathy and a great desire to help. Prominent people willingly offered their services, and the great Mark Twain himself, then one of the most popular writers in America, was to address a large meeting at Carnegie Hall in New York, leaving his packed audience with the moving words: "Remember San Francisco, the stricken city."

The press of most states and large cities carried headlines on the Disaster. It was top news in places as far apart as Oregon, Salt Lake City, Portland, Chicago, New York, Washington, D.C., and the largest and most striking of all the headlines appeared at Los Angeles, San Francisco's own great neighbor.

Nearer home, the Bay area had troubles of its own, but it was ready to help as soon as people saw how much misery the fire was causing in the city. The first ferry loads to cross the Bay brought people half mad with terror and the agony of fear. The earthquake had shaken the city from its very foundations and appalled the inhabitants. They had not had time to recover from the tremblor before the heat and crackle of uncontrolled fire unnerved them even more. The first instinct was to get away from it if they possibly could, and since nothing in San Francisco seemed safe any more, the idea of crossing the Bay, with the sea a safe barrier against the flames, was wonderfully welcome.

The great length of the San Andreas fault naturally affected many of the towns that lay alongside it while it was in movement. In addition to Stanford there was also great damage at San Jose and Santa Rosa (it was from the latter place that Jack London returned almost thankfully to San Francisco). The shock also affected the country districts. There it had happened at milking time, with the result that men and cows spilled on the ground, to be thrown time and again as they tried to rise. A story was told of a man riding a mule in front of a country store which collapsed as they passed. The sagacious mule promptly took the man home but could never again be persuaded to pass that store. Treetops all over the area waved wildly, and many white oaks and other trees were uprooted. Waves in the ground two or three feet in height and resembling the waves of the sea were reported from many directions. The fault passes under the sea for a considerable distance, and ships felt the shock with the sharp sensation that they had run aground and were beginning to drag over soft ground.

In San Rafael the Honorable William W. Morrow, circuit judge and president of the Red Cross, lived in a house surrounded by trees where, as he said, the birds in spring were numerous, busy, and noisy. On the morning of April 18th he awoke as the clock struck five and noticed that the day was bright and clear, the air fragrant and balmy. He lay in bed going over in his mind the engagements of the day when suddenly there broke upon the morning air the deep and ominous rumble of an earthquake. Suddenly it shook the house like a cyclone. It seemed to have the force and fury of a giant first from northeast, then from southwest, then vertical, then shaking and twisting the house like a demon. He felt another lesser shock at six o'clock and smaller ones later—on much the same pattern as those reported in San Francisco. Undeterred, the judge went as usual to the railway depot at 7:30 for the morning train to San Francisco. There was a small crevice in the ground at the San Rafael train depot. At Sausalito the depot was almost demolished. Whatever engagements Mr. Morrow had been reviewing as he lay peacefully in bed that morning, it was certain that his work with the Red Cross would occupy him for many days to come.

Eastward across the Bay, Oakland and Berkeley, farther away from the fault, escaped the scale of damage caused at San Francisco, and though many buildings were found to be unsafe they instantly became the principal reception centers for refugees from the city.

Seen by a young bride who had lived in Oakland for only a few weeks, the refugee influx came as the climax of sadness to a sequence of personal terror. Mrs. Shields had never previously experienced a tremor, and when she and her husband were awakened, as it seemed, in the middle of the night by the house shaking and bits falling off it, the girl could not understand what was happening. However, they quickly got up, dressed, and went out into their garden where their faithful Chinese servants—to whom *minor* earthquakes were nothing new—carried bedding out to the stables and laid it on the floor so that Mr. and Mrs. Shields might sleep there. All available canned food was also taken into the garden, where a cooking stove was quickly organized. Fully awake now, the bride found the secondary shocks far more alarming than the first. With each successive one she was in mortal terror lest it should be even more severe and that her house would come tumbling right down. Happily that was not the case, but when night came the sky was blood-red across the miles of the Bay from the awful fires raging in ruined San Francisco, and very soon every available place in their garden and stables was full of their escaping friends. Refugees poured past the windows, and husband and wife had their first quarrel on their account. Mrs. Shields' heart was moved to intense pity by the sight of those wretched people, and when a poor, sad-looking woman came by, holding two children by the hand, she felt she must help her.

There were no more blankets left to offer, so she caught up a valuable fur rug that had been one of her wedding presents and impulsively gave it to the sad little family. Her husband was very cross with her; but she told him that, though she might be young and foolish not to have thought of the value of the rug, she would certainly never regret helping those poor people who had no home to go to.

A boy named Donald McLaughlin who lived in Berkeley, eight miles across the Bay, particularly noticed what strange-looking people were the first refugees to cross over from San Francisco. But it was hardly surprising that they looked queer to a child who had never before witnessed the tragic scene of people taking refuge from terror—a sight which is all too well known to many European children today. It also seemed strange to him that none of his parents' friends arrived until all the best accommodation was already full, for he did not realize that many of them had remained on in the city to do what they could to help. When night came he watched the crimson clouds across the Bay while San Francisco was burning. The scene was theatrical and dramatic enough to impress his childish imagination, though he never noticed the magical sign which people said they saw in the sky when the fire was at its height. That sign, so it was said, was in the form of a cross formed by huge pillars of smoke coming from different directions, and many people, in their despairing fear, found comfort to see it there.

There were about 450,000 persons in San Francisco on the morning of the Disaster. Many of them were visitors and some, fortunately for themselves, managed to get away from the burning city if only by walking until their feet were blistered and bruised by the unaccustomed exercise. Other travelers were still arriving at San Francisco unaware of the terror that would meet them. Several ships entered the Bay on their ordinary occasions and on one of them was a boy who had made the voyage with his mother and father. To young Hulbert the scene was extraordinarily exciting and quite impersonal—just as television horrors are to the children of 1959. He thoroughly enjoyed the adventure though his parents were not so enthusiastic.

Another party that reached San Francisco that morning was very differently composed. Up in a hotel in the Pacific Heights district an impresario was staying. He had come on in advance to make arrangements for his burlesque troop, who had been engaged to perform at the theatre in San Francisco. They were due to arrive on April 18th, and he had promised to meet them at the railway station at Oakland and conduct them over on the ferry into the city. But on the morning of the earthquake—and also the morning of the arrival of the troupe—the manager was ill in bed and a young Frenchman of sixteen volunteered to go and meet the girls. It was a long and perilous journey—very different from what he had anticipated—and the troupe he met at the train was different too. It was made up of a bevy of beauties dressed in the height of fashion—the huge feathered hats, the sweeping skirts all in the brightest possible theatrical colors. The teen-ager got them all safely across to the city and then, as there were no conveyances, walked them gingerly up the middle of Market Street, for by then the sidewalks were impassable. He was greatly embarrassed not only by the terrible conditions into which the visitors had landed, but also by the girls themselves, who were so spectacular that they attracted maximum attention from the throngs of people in the broken streets.

There was another visitor who arrived that morning but who, unlike the rest, did not try to get away. Mr. Shields' brother, a well-known surgeon in New York, had seen much active service in the Philippine wars. The moment he got news of the Disaster he rushed to San Francisco with the humane idea of giving his services to the hundreds who must, he felt sure, be injured and dying there. His brother met him, and as he was a real estate man with a pass into the city (no one could enter without one after the fire had become a conflagration), the two men were able to get a passage over on the ferry. Mr. Shields was lucky enough to find an open democrat carriage outside the ferry, and in this he and his brother drove slowly along Market Street. But by that time the sights to be seen there were so terrible, so heart-rending, and so revolting that the hardened surgeon soldier vomited into the street as he saw the tragedy of San Francisco. His experiences in war made him realize, as few others could, the pain, suffering, and fear that he saw there.

In the end about 50,000 people were to be shipped across the Bay to friendly Oakland which, in spite of its own troubles, was quite ready to do its best for them, and thousands more were lodged elsewhere in the Bay area. But of the vast number of people to be provided for, the majority slept under the stars. During that first chaotic day they had tended to cluster listlessly in any large open space they could find. More and more slight shocks kept on occurring, and in the ever-present fear an open space seemed the safest place to be found in the city.

In San Francisco's desperate battle against the elements, earth, fire and water appeared the strongest and the most to be feared, but it was air, the famous little San Francisco wind, that was the most treacherous enemy of all. All through the morning of that first day firemen hoped against hope to be able to subdue the fires. But always the wind fanned the flames back to life again and gradually spread them farther and farther across the city. It was not easy for people who had been so fearfully awakened from their sleep, all unprepared for the ordeal that lay before them, to fight back, against torrid heat and smoke and amidst the intermittent explosions of dynamite which might at any moment mean that the house of any one of them had been destroyed in an effort to check the fire. Ruin stared men in the face that day; but it was impossible to think of personal loss in the general peril, and fortunately there were many brave and courageous men in San Francisco who possessed the same vision and determination as Mayor Schmitz.

The efforts of the brave and loyal staff of the Mint saved one of San Francisco's most famous and beautiful buildings, at first reported lost. Frank A. Leach, the superintendent, lived across the Bay, where he duly felt the earthquake; not particularly alarmed, he started at once for the city. On landing from the ferry he found that the place was in charge of the military. They had never heard of Mr. Leach, were disinclined to trust anything he said, and tried to prevent him from going farther. Happily he found a policeman who knew him, and was then allowed to go on at his own risk. When he arrived at the Mint building he found about fifty employees already mobilized to defend it, and he joined in the terrific battle that went on all that first day to prevent the Mint itself (said to have contained at that time $200,000,000 in gold and bullion) from catching fire from the buildings flaming all around it. There was a sea of fire on every side for seven terrible hours and it was only by the most careful watch on falling cinders that the danger was averted by five o'clock, though afterward a careful watch was kept all night long. The Mint was fortunate in having its own water supply, the installation of which had been completed only ten days before the Disaster. All the tanks in the roof (connected by pipes to the rest of the building) were fed from an artesian well in the courtyard worked by a strong pump, so that there was no lack of water for fighting the fire. As, by Leach's own admission, the fight was nevertheless so long and fierce, the danger from the surrounding fires can easily be imagined and by comparison the plight of other, less fortunate buildings readily understood.

Another brave public official was Arthur Fish, the postmaster of San Francisco. At first the beautiful new Post Office of which he had charge was said to be completely destroyed, but he refused to accept rumor as fact and fought his way through the debris of the street to find that the main building was still safe though the ornamentation had fallen off and some parts of it had been wrecked. Fish was a man with a high sense of public duty and he quickly set about the formidable task of getting the mails moving. It took him some days to establish perfect order, but it was done in a miraculously short time in view of the immense difficulties that confronted him. Moreover, his duty was done while he must have been in a state of extreme private anxiety. His family was in great danger, and his wife had been carried over to Oakland in order to save her life. For days it was impossible for him to get across the Bay to see her, but he never hesitated to put his public responsibilities before his private troubles. The stories of Leach and Postmaster Fish were only two of the thousands of stories of men's courage during the deadly dangerous emergency, but they were typical of many, told and untold, of the people of San Francisco.

The proclamation of Mayor Schmitz made an order that all looters were to be shot on sight, and this was invaluable in the prompt preservation of public order. In addition, when he heard that expressmen were charging $30 a load to haul goods— a rate quite prohibitive for poor people—he again acted immediately. "Tell your men," said the Mayor, "to seize all the wagons of such would-be extortionists and make use of them for the public good. The question of recompense will be seen to later." The Mayor and his volunteers, many of them members of the most distinguished families in San Francisco, were the brains of the relief work, and their example attracted many offers from people who were ready and willing to sally out and risk their lives in the flames to rescue the sick and dying. Hospitals were soon crowded, and nurses and doctors worked round the clock, but the spirit of the people called for the admiration of the world.

Meanwhile the fire rushed inexorably on and the heat from the mass of burning buildings was terrible beyond description. On the whole, people waited as long as they could before finally abandoning their homes and possessions. Then they literally ran for their lives in the dense smoky atmosphere that heralded the advancing flames. Then the streets they had left were completely empty except for an abandoned pile of luggage here and there, or a cart that had broken down under the too-heavy load that had been piled upon it—pathetic inanimate objects standing out against the smoke-dark sky, abandoned by people whose lives were no longer safe.

One of the peculiar features of the conflagration was that in many cases tall buildings showed the first signs of fire from their top stories while the lower ones remained apparently unscathed. One explanation was that the inside was on fire and that pressure had built up until the flames broke out at the top—a sensible enough theory but one that did not immediately occur to people who had come to think of the fire as something alive, supernatural, and demoniac. Neither can it have been the only explanation, for James Stetson, whose office was at 123 California Street, had a personal experience which contradicted it. He was anxious to reach his room in order to rescue his papers and so, as naturally no elevator was working, he started off slowly up the stairs. Although there seemed to be no smoke in the building, he encountered a shower of sparks on the stairs. The sparks appeared to come from the fifth floor where, he soon discovered, the building was already burning merrily. He hastily came down again and he afterward said that he was in the midst of a "perfect firestorm." Possibly broken gas mains on the ground floor had caused the gas to mount suddenly and ignite at the top; but, whatever the reason, top-floor fires were a common sight in San Francisco that day. To the nervous, overwrought citizens the sight of flames bursting from top-story windows when there was no sign of fire at the bottom seemed weird and unnatural; already there were people who said that the Disaster was an act of God to punish the place for its wickedness, and top-floor fires seemed to show that this was no ordinary conflagration but something beyond human understanding.

General Funston, the man who had seen the beginning of the fire from Nob Hill and who had risked the anger of his military superiors by acting on his own initiative and calling out the soldiers to help San Francisco, worked on without respite and soon became personally familiar to firemen, police, and everyone engaged in relief. On the whole his military despotism worked well and in general people only knew of its beneficence. For the troops had no need to use much violence. A few scattered rifle-shots from the men in uniform, a few blows from rifle butts, and the city became more law-abiding than ever in its history. A sort of crowd psychology never before seen in San Francisco, a free and easy town if ever there was one, seemed to decree respect for the rights of the public.

In addition to the Federal troops under Funston, Pardee, the Governor of California, called in the National Guard (the state force under his orders) to help, and six hundred cadets of the University of California also went into action on the orders of President Wheeler.

Help also came from the sea, and every tanker that happened to be in the Bay neighborhood immediately made for San Francisco in order to offer assistance. And the President of the United States, Theodore Roosevelt, as soon as he heard of the desperate plight of the city, wired his sympathy and pledged the help of the Navy. Being a wise man,

138

and knowing the generous hearts of Americans, he begged publicly that the considerable aid which the nation would certainly offer should be entrusted, for proper administration, to the good offices of the Red Cross.

Pitiful cries from the burning city called aloud for "bread, bread, bread." The Mayor sent a desperate telegram to the women of Los Angeles asking them in the name of heaven to bake bread at once and deliver it at their Chamber of Commerce, whence it would be immediately rushed up to San Francisco. Governor Pardee appealed to the Mayor of Los Angeles himself. "For God's sake," he wired, "rush all available cooked food to San Francisco as soon as possible. I will see that the trains are rushed through."

The President's order to the Navy was promptly and punctiliously obeyed. The fireboats *Active* and *Leslie* with all available hose and a supply of dynamite were sent to San Francisco by Admiral McCalla, while the Red Cross ship *Prebble* dashed to the city with surgeons, nurses, and medical supplies. Bluejacket fire fighters from the Navy took charge on the waterfront and helped to save the ferries so that they might maintain the vital outlet to Oakland, Berkeley, Alameda, and Sausalito for the thousands of refugees crossing the Bay to escape the wall of flame that surrounded them.

139

Many civilian volunteers helped the sailors and during the whole ordeal they took an active part in the titanic struggle.

Always, all the time, there were long lines of patient people vainly waiting, hour after hour, to try to get messages out to their loved ones in other parts of America. But San Francisco had to stand alone; it was all but impossible to get private news in or out of the city, and frightened men and women had to do without the comfort of communication with their families during their great ordeal. The one serviceable wire was reserved for public use, and in desperation Western Union sent no less than five thousand messages from Los Angeles to San Francisco by *train*. These messages had a better chance of arriving than had transcontinental ones, for the Southern Pacific Railway Company had a railhead from Los Angeles in the city itself, whereas all continental traffic had to arrive from Oakland via the ferry, in the same way as it did until recently. And it was those transcontinental messages that were the most important, for terrifying rumors were spreading about the plight of San Francisco. It was said that at least a thousand people had been killed by the earthquake alone— an exaggeration which must have caused great anxiety to relatives of people living in the burning, isolated city.

The casualty figures were happily exaggerated, but the truth about the plight of San Francisco was grim enough. The two mighty elements of earth and fire worked closely together throughout that terrible day, the one beginning what the other was threatening to complete. From under collapsed buildings rescuers had to listen appalled to cries of anguish from victims roasting to death in the prison to which the earthquake had condemned them. The city had been half knocked down and fire was everywhere. Rarely had such a disaster been recorded in the history of the human race.

SEVEN

THE classical canvas of the Disaster was set off by the small personal incidents with which it was colored and which were typical of the spirit of the people of San Francisco.

Thus, Mr. Shields' sight-seeing expedition in his brand-new automobile not only showed their coolness in the face of the greatest earthquake ever known, but also illustrated a certain gay and lively quality inseparable from the life of the city. A catastrophe had happened which must bring the social life so dear to their hearts to an end for the time being. But people felt that they must have a look at the damage before it was cleared away.

After vainly trying to collect Ethel McAllister's old great-aunt from the Hotel Bella Vista, Mr. Shields' party went on down Market Street to see the fire. The flames, which no one at that time doubted would soon be put out by their famous Fire Force, provided a spectacle not to be missed. Mr. Shields stopped his automobile opposite the Palace Hotel, and there, before long, his carload had all the excitement they could have wished for. It was more than one lady could stand and she was reduced to screaming hysterics. For while they were actually looking on from the other side of the street the fierce fire that had been contained within the walls of the sumptuous building suddenly burst out from the windows with a tremendous roar, and flames poured into the street.

At that point Mr. Shields thought it would be prudent, as well as necessary, to drive elsewhere. Curiously enough, he made no move to take Ethel and the rest of the party home or to give up sight-seeing. Instead they drove toward Union Square, but had only got as far as Grant when he found that they had no more gasoline and so came to a full stop. Whereupon one of the elder ladies took the opportunity to lead her hysterical friend gently homeward, feeling, no doubt, that they had had enough. Mr. Shields and the other gentleman went off in a long search for more gasoline while Ethel was left sitting quietly in the car, alone.

The time was two o'clock and Ethel sat there by herself until five. During those three long hours she was not frightened, as well she might have been, and she certainly did not lack for company. After a while a small boy about nine years old came wandering along, his small face pinched, his eyes starting out of his head at all the sights he had seen. Noticing a young girl sitting alone in an automobile and perhaps feeling the need to talk to someone, he went up to Ethel and began to tell her about his experiences. At the first earthquake shock his home in the Mission District had been destroyed and the inhabitants scattered. From that time he was a lost little boy without parents and without friends. He had simply walked and walked until he found himself in Union Square, and for the life of him he did not know what to do or where to go next.

Ethel, resourceful though she undoubtedly was, hardly knew what to suggest. Then, to her enormous relief, a couple came along and asked if they could help. They seemed to her to be curious-looking people and were dressed in anything but conservative clothes. She felt sure that they must be actors from one of the companies in San Francisco's theatres. But they were kind, and at that grim moment that was all that mattered. They smiled cheerfully at the little boy, took his hand, and led him away to camp with them for the night in Union Square, promising that next morning they would try to help him find his parents.

One more adventure befell Ethel during that long wait in the empty car while the flames were never very far away. A frantic clerk, apparently crazed with fear, came tearing up to one of the shuttered shops just across the road and beat frantically on the door. When he got no reply—which was hardly strange in the circumstances—he cried and moaned, "What shall I do, what shall I do? I work there and they won't let me in." In his distraught state he was quite unable to grasp that no business was being done in the city that day. Finally, in spite of his struggles, he was swept away in the moving, swaying crowd, still crying and protesting about the refusal of his employers to let him in. He was lost to the girl's sight, but his misery left a poignant impression on her and she was thankful when soon afterward Mr. Shields and his friend came back carrying a little precious gasoline which they had been lucky enough to get hold of after a walk of several difficult miles. The car got going again and before long Ethel was safely home, where she found her mother beginning to get very anxious about her safety.

Personal safety, and indeed the very continuity of life itself were uppermost in people's minds that day. For engaged couples it seemed imperative that they should be married at once while there

145

was still time. Perhaps it might have been supposed that they would have other matters to occupy them, but the fact remains that there was never such a rush for marriage licenses in the history of San Francisco as on the day of the Disaster, when they were issued at the rate of seven every hour. Happily for the romantic and apprehensive couples who wished to marry, one of the clerks from the totally destroyed City Hall had thought of rescuing the book of license blanks, thus saving all concerned from an embarrassing and difficult situation.

The rescue of the marriage license blanks had an echo in the brave action of another citizen, Colonel Murphy. When he heard that the Commercial High School was burning and that there was no hope of saving it, on his own initiative he at once fought his way through to the building. Unlike the frantic refugees who in the mental confusion of shock rescued all sorts of useless things from the ruin of their homes, Murphy knew just what he was after, and that was no less than ninety-three typewriters—probably the school's most valuable asset. With infinite difficulty he somehow managed to get all the machines away to safety, and it was actually on those same typewriters that high school students eventually typed out letters to send all over the world telling of the city's plight and asking help in raising a six-million-dollar fund for rebuilding San Francisco's schools.

146

Murphy was lucky in being allowed to enter the burning high school. Captain Harts, an Engineer officer in the Army, was less fortunate. He went down the hill from his house into the burning city but was refused admission to his office because he was not in uniform. There was nothing for it but to walk home again, change, and for a second time make his way downtown. He was kept busy most of the day, helping where he could, and at one time he was put in charge of the dynamiting of buildings. All the same he managed to get home in time to take his little daughter, Polly, up onto the hill opposite to where they lived, and from there they saw the St. Francis Hotel burn for the second time in its history. It was awe-inspiring and terrible as each floor in turn was consumed and fell amid a towering mass of sparks and flames. How wonderful to watch when one is safe!

But was anyone really safe in that oppressively dangerous city? The first earthquake shock, though extremely grave in its consequences and horribly alarming in its impact, was something from which the town could recover. So too, it was thought, were the fires which, at first small in scale, could fairly easily be put out. But after it was realized that there was no water for the firemen's hoses a different and literally more lurid light shone upon the whole Disaster. It became something which affected everyone and which might go on and on until the whole splendid city was ruined and the citizens with it.

Market Street ran diagonally across the town from the Ferry Building, and gradually it began to appear as though the whole of the town southeast of that street would be destroyed, and what then? Was there any hope of saving anything? Could the rushing, crackling, torrid flames ever be arrested? No one could say, but everyone began to fear that San Francisco's ordeal was far from over. The fire was said to be attacking a house every minute, and soon the beautiful, wicked billows of smoke rose five miles into the air. Against that theatrically macabre background the parts of the city still standing were outlined in black and white, with the blue sky of California still defiantly challenging the darkness of the burning area.

But, in spite of it all, people were remarkably calm. There were still many about the streets in their night clothes, puzzled, bewildered, and not knowing where to go, but accepting their ordeal without panic. Men were dirty and unshaven, and children who at first enjoyed the thrilling adventure were becoming tired and disagreeable. The day passed better for anyone who had a job to do, and Elmer Enewold, having shut off the gas "which was pouring out like sixty" from the broken mains into his home, cleaned up the three-inch layer of soot from a fallen chimney which covered the kitchen, and then reported to the Armory to see what he could do. He was forced to leave his mother and sisters behind—his father was out of town—but they were very cool and, like him, felt that he should give a hand in the emergency.

Elmer was at once enrolled in a band of sixty volunteers and told to go out and mount guard over the Broadway Street jail. Taking care to keep to the middle of the street they went at the double through that blazing hell of flying glass and bricks, "lickety-cut." At first they were kept busy breaking into saloons and putting the liquor out into the middle of the streets where it could be collected by the military, and generally keeping order where necessary.

Useless fire engines lay about the streets in a mass of blackened machinery, and the flames seemed to be laughing at the helpless firemen. By their light Elmer managed to scribble a note and send it to his family telling them in his cheerful way that he was still "alive and kicking," but that once having volunteered for a job he could not get home again. By three o'clock on the morning of the 19th the flames were so close to the jail he was guarding that drastic action had to be taken. The officials' first idea was to turn all prisoners loose, and rumors got about that criminals and madmen were mixing with the crowds in the streets. But the band of helpers offered to try to deliver the prisoners to Fort Mason, though there were three hundred desperate men against sixty volunteers. All the murderers and violent cases were handcuffed to a long chain while the others were made to form up and march between the thin line of guards. After four hours' marching most of them reached Fort Mason, but inevitably some prisoners made a successful dash for freedom and were lost in the dawdling, aimlessly swaying crowds.

During the first day of the fire the wind, though it undoubtedly helped to fan the flames, had been light. But, as though air perceived that its efforts to help earth and fire were not great enough, the situation changed on the second day. Then the wind suddenly became variable, coming now from one quarter and now from another, thus adding enormously to the difficulties of the fire fighters. There were three thousand refugees crowded into Jefferson Square, and when the fire reached as far as the corner of it they were near to panic. The hot breath of the flames reached out toward them, crackling and roaring as they came. There seemed no way of escape for the wretched homeless ones who had already lost everything but their lives. "But by the will of God," said Enewold, "the wind died down and the fire at that corner died out. Otherwise there

would have been an awful loss of life." A near miracle saved the lives of those lying under the stars.
But they could not sleep. They had no shelter at all,
and little or no covering, and with morning the
characteristic San Francisco fog came up over the
city, with no precipitation to help extinguish the fire
but damp enough to make the air cold and horribly uncomfortable for the campers.

Young Enewold had some exciting and terrifying
experiences during his time as a volunteer. At one
moment he saw a man bending over something on
the ground and, having yelled at him without effect,
fired a shot as they had all been told to do. To his
relief he missed, but when the man started to run
another shot from the other side of the street rang
out and the man, a Negro, toppled over. No one
then had time to think about burial any more
than have soldiers on a battlefield, and the corpse of
the looter was simply thrown into the burning ruins.
He had been after the body of a man half buried
under a heap of bricks, thinking, no doubt, that he
had valuables or jewels about him.

By Thursday afternoon all the city's stock of dynamite had been used. It seemed to the tired and
desperate firemen, now stripped of their only remaining weapon of defense, that there was no reason why the fire should not blaze away until the

whole city was consumed. No water for the hoses, no dynamite to blow up houses in the van of the fire in order to make a space large enough to stop it. What more could they do? They had provisionally marked down Van Ness Avenue as a suitable place in which to make a last effort to stop the flames from reaching the western part of the city. The handsome avenue was a hundred and ten feet wide, and full of rich men's houses (instead of the automobile showrooms that stand there today), and it seemed that if enough houses on the Market Street side could be demolished there might be a good chance that the fire would not be able to cross the avenue and attack the other side. After a pause of desperation, the firemen started lighting more backfires behind Van Ness, hoping against hope to clear a space in that way. But before too long their friends in the Navy brought in more dynamite, and battle could be joined again on more equal terms.

In spite of the rapidly worsening situation there were still people who kept cheerful. A handsomely dressed woman with two children was heard to say gallantly: "I have money if I could get it and use it. I have friends if I could get to them. Meanwhile I am going to cook this piece of bacon on these bricks I have found and be happy."

The headlines of newspapers on the 19th hardly helped to allay the general fear:

ENTIRE CITY OF SAN FRANCISCO IN
DANGER OF BEING ANNIHILATED
PANIC STRICKEN PEOPLE FLEE
THEATERS RUINED
RESIDENCES BURNING
DEAD IN STREET
DAMAGE A BILLION
MARTIAL LAW DECLARED

The last, owing to prompt action by Funston and
the Mayor and because of the good spirit of the
majority of the citizens, was not true. Martial law
was never necessary in San Francisco during that
long ordeal.

The *Oakland Times* carried banner headlines
no less than two and a half inches high—surely a
record for the time—crying aloud:

SAN FRANCISCO DESTROYED
STARVING TO DEATH
PEOPLE SHOT DOWN IN STREETS OF
SAN FRANCISCO

Small wonder that a friend of Mr. and Mrs.
Frank Symmes of Berkeley, after she at length received a wire assuring her of their safety, sent
them a postal card telling them that, since receiving it, and only then, had she looked at the papers.
"I think," she wrote, "it would almost have driven
me crazy if I had read them before. . . . We feel
as if nothing else mattered much now we know you
are safe."

153

EXTRA THE DAILY NEWS EXTRA

VOL 7. NO. 25. FOURTH YEAR. SAN FRANCISCO, WEDNESDAY EVENING, APRIL 18, 1906. INDEPENDENT. 25c MONTH; 4 COPY.

HUNDREDS DEAD!

Fire Follows Earthquake, Laying Downtown Section in Ruins--City Seems Doomed
For Lack of Water

KNOWN DEAD

AT MECHANICS' PAVILION

Max Fenner, policeman, killed in collapse Essex Hotel.

Niece of Detective Dillon, killed in collapse, 6th and Shipley.

Unidentified woman, killed at 18 7th st.

Two unknown men, brought in autos.

OTHER DEAD

Five killed, 2 injured, in collapse of building at 239 Geary.

Frank Corali, buried, beneath basement floor of burning lodging house 5th and Mission. Heard crying "For God's sake, help me."

Seven firemen killed in collapse of brick power house Valencia and 7th.

John Wheley and son, killed in falling house, Steiner and Germania ave.

James Whaley, wife. Nellie Whaley, Marie Whaley, same address, badly injured.

Unidentified man, buried in remains Valencia-st. Hotel.

At 8.40 there were 100 dead and dying at the Pavilion, one more arriving each minute.

Miss Katt Brown, a niece of Detective Dillon.

At 126 Langton, 4 killed; Billy Sheehan, policeman, rescued 3 people.

Many injured at 117 6th st., Hotel Phillips.

San Francisco was practically desolated and totally paralyzed by the earthquake, which commenced at 5:11 a.m. today and continued with terrific vigor for four minutes.

Great loss of life was caused by the collapse of buildings, and many people met a most cruel death by fire. Flames broke out in all parts of the city.

The monetary loss caused by the earthquake, the fires which followed it and the depreciation in values that will result will amount to hundreds of millions of dollars.

The progress of San Francisco has received a check from which it will probably take many years to recover.

Thousands of men who went to bed wealthy last night awoke this morning practically bankrupt.

The fury of the temblor was greater than any that has been known in the history of the city.

The people are appalled, terror-stricken. Thousands, fearful of a recurrence of the dreadful disaster, with results still more dire, are hastening out of San Francisco.

Many heart-rending scenes have been enacted. Families are moving their belongings helter-skelter, and moving aimlessly about, keeping in the open.

The City Hall is a complete wreck. The walls surrounding the grand dome have fallen, leaving only the skeleton frame work and the top of the dome intact. Around all sides of the building the walls have crumbled, like so many cards. The Receiving Hospital was buried.

The surgeons moved to Mechanics' Pavilion, which today is a combined hospital and morgue. Dead and dying are brought in by autos, ambulances and even garbage carts.

Insane patients were taken from the Emergency Hospital to Mechanics' Pavilion. Many of them were hurt. Some broke loose and ran among the dying, adding horror to the scene.

At 8:15 a second sharp quake occurred, accentuating the terror.

The horror attending following the earthquake, was and are fearful to behold. Had the earthquake occurred an hour later, the entire city would have burnt into ruins.

At least forty buildings were aflame within ten minutes after the temblor passed. Among the first to go were the buildings on Market, Battery, Sansome, First, Second, Third, Fourth, Fifth, and Sixth streets, followed by a general conflagration Francisco Bay.

A building collapsed at Steiner and Haight sts. No report of loss of life.

Along Market st. from 5th toward Castro, the sidewalks are literally strewn with wreckage. In many places the sidewalks have collapsed, falling into the basements.

This is true on Market between 5th and 6th, between 6th and 7th, and between 7th and City Hall Square, on the west side.

There are probably not fifty chimneys standing in the city. This means that many more fires are to be expected, as fires are cracked everywhere.

A small portion of the front of the West Side Christian Church was shaken out.

St. Ignatius' Church was badly shaken but is intact. Great damage resulted at St. Ignatius college, a portion of the building being destroyed.

A building was burned at the end of California street, in the Richmond.

Concordia Club, Van Ness Ave., badly dismantled.

At the Cosmopolitan Hotel, Fifth and Mission sts., fire is believed to have killed a number of people. The building was totally destroyed.

St. Winifred's hospital, Sutter near Larkin, was injured, but is intact.

At 9:30 the following were at Mechanics' Pavilion. But few were dead, although the injuries of many were reported as fatal:

Mrs Jones, 509 Stevenson; M R D Wells, 314 Van Ness; Wm Castro, roy, 410 14 Natoma; Bernard Atchison; 159 3rd; Ernest Edner 1143 Mission; Bert Kennedy, 372 Howard; Geo Sullivan, 313 O G ave; Geo Menworth, 334 4th; Philip Hendes, 3 Eddy; Wm Gamman, 112 4th; D J Erchon, 172 7th; Geo Rengone, 94 Folsom; Cornfield, 939 1-2 Folsom; Wm Carr, 15474 Ellis; Wm Anderson, 1293 Market; F Butler, 137 6th; R Walsworth, 111 Geary; J Justice, Brunswick House; J Hart, Los Angeles; H Young, 1874 16th ave; Lou Vittery, 909 Kearny; V Dedard, 149 Turk: Belle McDonald, 2512 Stevenson; Obal Marshall, 149 Turk. A H Peterson, 234 1-2 Natoma. R H Lauder, 7th and Howard, Brunswick House.

THEATER WRECKED

The Majestic Theater is almost a complete wreck, the rear and, on the 7th st side, having fallen out, while the roof caved

---

Wells Fargo Bank History Room, San Francisco

The "Daily News" of April 18, 1906. This was the only paper published in the city on the day of the disaster

---

In spite of alarmist headlines in some papers, the share taken by the press in helping to establish some sort of order and security in the tortured city could hardly be overestimated. One of the things that caused most distress to people who were virtually imprisoned in the burning city was their inability to get in touch with their families outside. In order to help as best they could, the newspapers daily carried whole pages of small advertisements from private persons seeking to communicate with their friends and relatives. Ordinarily the charge for such a service would have been relatively high, but during the emergency no one was required to pay.

Another generous action by the press was that of the *Globe* newspaper of Boston, Massachusetts. Boston, like so many other American cities, early realized that what was happening in San Francisco was far beyond the range of ordinary tragedy, and it resolved to do what it could to help. *People in San Francisco or anywhere in territory affected by the great calamity,* ran the notice in the paper, *are urged to notify their friends in the east of their safety and present address through the Boston* Globe. *Telegraph at the expense of the Boston* Globe. But of course in the devastated city no telegraph was usable by private individuals.

Placards were posted at the Ferry Building, where they would be seen by all seeking to cross the Bay, describing missing members of families—like that of the little boy who appealed to Ethel McAllister—in case any who passed by might be able to help in finding them. In addition to placards describing the missing there were notices listing a number of *don'ts* for citizens. These were up all over

Headquarters
Health Commission
TO THE PUBLIC
Food and Water Consumption

1. ALL WATER SHOULD BE BOILED, WHETHER FOR DRINKING, BATHING OR CLEANSING PURPOSES.

USE NO UNBOILED WATER IN THE PREPARATION OF FOOD FOR COOKING OR BAKING.

USE UNBOILED WATER ONLY FOR FLUSHING PURPOSES.

THIS ORDER APPLIES TO ALL WATER, WHETHER SPRING VALLEY, LAKE OR WELL WATER.

2. ALL MILK SHOULD BE BOILED, WHETHER USED BY INFANTS OR ADULTS.

3. FOOD IN CANS SHOULD NOT BE ALLOWED TO STAND UNCOVERED, LEST IT BECOME TAINTED OR INFECTED.

4. DO NOT EAT UNCOOKED VEGETABLES.

5. ALL BUTCHER SHOPS AND BAKERIES SHOULD BE SCREENED.

6. ALL CANNED GOODS SHOULD BE COOKED.

BY ORDER OF

DR. JAMES M. WARD,
SIGNED: PRESIDENT HEALTH COMMISSION.

DR. D. F. RAGAN,
HEALTH OFFICER.

PHILLIPS & VAN ORDEN CO., SAN FRANCISCO, CAL.

Wells Fargo Bank History Room, San Francisco

THE FIGHT AGAINST EPIDEMICS

the city on any wall still standing, and a sample of their advice was DON'T USE HOUSE TOILET UNDER ANY CIRCUMSTANCES—USE CHLORIDE OF LIME OR SOME OTHER GOOD DISINFECTANT. Problems of sanitation were alarmingly difficult in the devastated city and rumors of pestilence were already circulating. They were never a fact, but among the refugees busy tongues talked of scarlet fever, typhus, and smallpox, adding yet more to the heavy load of anxiety.

Many of the splendid palaces on Van Ness Avenue had already been blown up and St. Mary's Roman Catholic Cathedral was doomed to the same fate. But the untiring efforts of its priest saved the church. With a gallantry like that of the London fire watchers in St. Paul's Cathedral in the 1940's, where everything around except the church itself was burned to the ground, the priest of St. Mary's in San Francisco climbed up to the roof and methodically and calmly extinguished every burning spark and particle that fell upon it. The private houses were all burned or blown up, but St. Mary's still stands today as a memorial to the courage of its priest.

The mass of people and carts that thronged Van Ness Avenue made many dread a stampede which would have turned a desperate situation into a holocaust. The situation was not helped by a fanatic who cried about the streets, "The Lord sent it, the Lord sent it," until people fell on their knees, imploring heaven for mercy and an end to their agony, and incidentally stopping the traffic on the crowded avenue. But the end of the "guilty" city's ordeal was not in sight. The fire seemed to be eating out the very heart of it as though in an effort to destroy its whole existence. For the patient, brave human beings who were forced to endure all that might come to them time moved on leaden feet. Their future was unpredictable in those tragic days and they felt condemned to an eternity of suffering. To the flames alone belonged the prerogative of rapid movement and they bounded triumphantly from place to place, filling the streets with unendurable heat and furious noise.

Day by day in that sublime, heroic time the queues for the ferry lengthened. All sorts of people stood there, rich and poor, society beauties and women from the Barbary Coast, waiting, waiting for their turn to cross the Bay into safety. There was little else for them to do. Behind them was the furnace, before them the blue of the sea promising escape. The people were grim-faced and for the most part silent, exhausted by their long ordeal. Some wore thick coats and some thin; underneath the coats many still had on the formal evening dress of the night of the opera, while some, caught in their beds by the earthquake, still wore nightdresses. Everyone was carrying something, and they were articles of a most curious variety. There were of course the untidy bundles inseparable from refugees fleeing from their homes in any part of the world. But in the San Francisco lines there was also a surprising number of bird cages. It seemed as though, just as people gave a last, despairing look around their living rooms, their canaries had let out a bright, jaunty song which impelled the owners to take the birds along with them rather than leave them to roast to death as the flames finally devoured the houses. There were also the inevitable pet dogs, yelping as they were trodden on by the milling, thoughtless crowds. The queues for the ferry were a kaleidoscope of suffering in those April days.

Every available horse carriage (and they scarcely existed once the soldiers moved in and started to commandeer) was piled up and crowded to capacity. Horses, however, could only go at walking pace because of the thousands of pedestrians who thronged the streets. One young man with a van going, as he hoped, to the ferry gave a lift to a handsome woman in a sealskin coat, whose face was black with smoke and whose hands were heavily bandaged. Their pace was so slow that they fell into conversation, and before long she unbound her left hand, which to his amazement was glittering and blazing with the white light of diamonds. Men's rings and ladies' rings covered every finger and even her thumb—rings much too large for her so that they were tied on with thread to prevent them from dropping off. The extraordinary sight not unnaturally made the man curious, and his passenger, talking freely, told him that she was the wife of a jeweler and that what she had with her was all that she had been able to rescue from their stock. Her handbag was also full of precious objects. She had worked so hard to save what she could from the wreckage of all they possessed and was so exhausted from picking her way over the rubble and piles of masonry in the streets that she would certainly have fallen and never reached the ferry at all had she not had the good fortune to get a lift. Whether her rescuer was ever suitably rewarded is not on record.

Rich men were jostling the very poor in those crowded lines at the ferry, for all social barriers were down. Though many of them owned valuable collections of jewels and priceless Fabergé ornaments, few had saved anything but old hats, umbrellas, and all sorts of junk. Wits were all at sea, reason all but gone; personal safety was all that mattered. So they went out, perhaps forever, with things which they did not prize at all but which had been easy to snatch up from their ruined homes.

A man dazed with grief was seen staggering along toward the ferry clutching a more than usually odd-looking bundle in his arms. He hung onto it as though it were his very life, but when kind hands sought to relieve him of the weight which he seemed scarcely able to bear they found inside the poor man's bundle the bodies of two dead babies.

160

Somehow he had hoped to be able to revive his children with the warmth of his own body; their mother had been killed in the earthquake and the babies were all he had left.

Had the ferry queues not been tragic they might have been laughable, not only because of the extremely odd appearance of people in the various stages of dress and undress, but also because of some amusing incidents. As the line moved slowly onto the ferryboat a man came aboard carrying a great big coop with a white rat in it. One of his fellow passengers had a good mind to kick the thing overboard, but he kindly refrained from doing so when the owner told him that the rat was no ordinary rodent. He was a performing rat; he came when called and would beg like a dog. In fact he was part of a turn, and people gathered around and begged the owner to give a performance while the ferry made the crossing of the Bay. The end of the story was never told, but in that jostling, brave, pathetic crowd of Californians, ready even then to laugh at anything that might take their minds off their desperate situation, it was perfectly possible that the rat was made to do his tricks for their amusement.

There must have been many Orientals alongside Americans in the ferry queues, for Chinatown had been wiped out by the combination of fire and earthquake. The parlor cribs, sumptuously furnished and heavily scented, had gone forever, and with them a feature of old San Francisco. Not that the Chinese used them—they could have their pick of the smuggled-in girls before they ever reached the cribs. But to many white men, strangers seeking their fortune in a strange land, the cribs and their occupants had seemed like paradise—and a fascinatingly different paradise from anything they had ever dreamed of. But they all vanished with the fire, and the girls and their masters were equal at last—all of them refugees waiting for the ferry.

By Friday firemen who had worked day and night since the first emergency in the early hours of Wednesday were tired out. From the moment they heard that the city's supply of dynamite was exhausted they were frustrated and desperate in the knowledge that they must fight the enormous danger to the town without water and without explosive.

Sullivan's young friend Rudi Schubert, after his long ordeal, surrounded by terror and the screams of dying men, determined to go off duty. He was very anxious about the fate of his young wife, whom he had not seen or heard of since the earthquake. They had been married for only six months and he longed to know if she was safe. He set out to walk toward the place that had been his home, but he did not realize how tired he was and he collapsed on a sidewalk unable to go any farther. Rudi remembered nothing more until he awoke inside a tent in the Presidio. A soldier had picked him up, sound asleep in the street, and had carried him off to safety.

It was lucky for him that he was taken to the Presidio, for there he heard news of his wife, who had been there before him but had moved on out into the country. When the Schuberts' lodgings in California Street looked like being burned out, Mrs. Schubert dressed herself, saved her husband's best bowler hat and their newly bought encyclopedia, and together with a friend (who for some unknown reason had on two nightdresses and nothing else) set out for safety. She had heard nothing of her husband but knew that he must be out with his crew somewhere in the blazing city, and her anxiety can be imagined. As for Rudi, once he knew that she was safe and had himself had a good sleep, he reported back for duty. He heard no more of his young wife for ten days.

By Friday morning the Relief Committee realized with some alarm that the matter of the disposal of corpses in the city was becoming urgent. In Chinatown, for instance, there were many bodies lying about the streets, and macabre stories were spreading among people in the frightened and bewildered city. One man picked up four corpses in Market Street and piled them onto his horse truck.

But as he went along a great building fell down in his path, and flames rushed through the gap it made chasing him as he fled and soon licking up both dead and living—man, horse, and bodies alike.

Fear of pestilence as well as ordinary human decency made it imperative that the dead should be buried, and Funston, ever on the alert, saw that he must act quickly and decisively before disease attacked the living through the putrefying bodies of the dead. He at once gave orders that every male person capable of handling a pick or shovel should dig for one hour, until the work was done. It was a grisly job, but men found even that a welcome respite from the endless waiting in those long days of trial. They dug deep trenches in the sand and soon all were decently if quickly buried. Funston's unquestioned authority had again prevailed.

Many people had succeeded in getting away from San Francisco, but countless thousands remained in the city, and for them, unless they could reach an official food station, life was very expensive. There were plenty of dishonest people who had managed to hide a store of food; and on the first days, before the food stations had had time to get properly organized, people were paying twenty-five cents for a small glass of mineral water, a dollar for a loaf of bread, a dollar apiece for eggs, and (if they were lucky enough to find one) fifty dollars for a cab to the ferry. Some enterprising person had the idea of killing and eating the ornamental ducks on Lake Merced and by Friday they were merrily cooking in the improvised kitchens. If any found their way to the street where young Leonora Chase lived she was no doubt delighted by the delicious smell.

There were still many prostitutes about the city, though the streets which were their normal stalking ground were all but empty. The sight of them stirred up some righteous indignation even among the tolerant San Franciscans, and at one time there was talk of lynching. But the city was accustomed to prostitution and the girls were left to get along as best they could in the ruins.

Once the roar of the fire had passed by, the streets were silent in their terrible isolation. One man, walking fearfully among the accumulated debris, trying to find the place that had once been his home, reported stumbling over a dead body with the head almost burned off—a corpse that had escaped the notice of Funston's diggers.

Huge tottering buildings loomed lonely against the sky, particularly around the ferry and Market Street. Days that should have been bright with sun were almost dark, and great beds of what seemed like coals, but were in fact remains of burned-out houses, gave out an enormous heat and glowed brightly when night fell. The air and the ground were hot from fire day and night, a particularly alarming sensation that can be readily understood by anyone who visited the burned-out streets of the City of London in 1941. There, in that one mile, the soles of shoes walking over the ground became unbearably hot weeks after the fire; in San Francisco the burned-out area was many times as large.

EIGHT

WHILE the word went out all over the American continent, and indeed the globe, to help San Francisco, the city authorities themselves never relaxed. Mayor Schmitz and his Relief Committee, ever on the move as the fire destroyed their meeting places, talked and slept little but thought much and to good purpose during that terrible time.

Funston, in command of a Federal, not a state force, was determined that the city should obtain all possible help from Washington. He sent a telegram to the Secretary of War, William H. Taft, asking for thousands of tents and all the rations that could be managed to be sent to San Francisco with the utmost possible speed. Taft acted promptly, for the great emergency in the western city was well understood, and before long enormous relief camps, composed of row upon row of tents, were set up in all suitable places—suitable, that is, because they seemed at a safe distance from the conflagration. The tented cities that appeared in the Presidio and the Golden Gate Park could accommodate 200,000 refugees; Jefferson Square, though not so safely isolated, also had its tents, as did any other large open space. Afterward, when the fire was out, tents were replaced by huge relief camps made up of long rows of wooden huts. And these remained in the city for nearly two years. Some may exist to this day, for eventually they were sold cheap to anyone who would buy and cart them away bodily to various parts of the state, where, no doubt, they continued to serve a useful purpose.

Extreme measures were at once taken to prevent plagues in the camps, and gallons of disinfectant were used. Medical people had their hands more than full if only because of the number of births in the refugee camps and even on the sands near Fort Mason. But with good will and hard work matters were kept well in hand and no one suffered too much. Drunkenness, which in those awful hours might well have been a problem, was virtually

GARBAGE

All householders and persons camping on Public squares or other places, are directed to remove all garbage and refuse from their premises to curb line of street for removal to crematory.

This rule must be observed in order to protect the health of the city.

DR. JAMES W. WARD
President Health Commission.

AN INSTRUCTION TO REFUGEE CAMPERS

eliminated by the Mayor's order that all saloons should be closed immediately. Thereafter liquor could be had only on a doctor's prescription, and private stocks were commandeered to remove temptation and to help doctors issue such prescriptions where necessary.

Humor never failed and jocular placards abounded:

THE FAIRMONT, THE UNFAIRMONT

And on a street sandwich cart:

MEALS A LA CART

FIRST TO SHAKE, FIRST TO BURN,
A LIVING TO EARN

Nor did the public spirit of San Francisco falter. On Friday April 20th, a bare two days after the earthquake, the *Oakland Examiner* carried the following in its leader:

"We are going to rebuild as soon as it can be done," said a store-keeper. That character is typical . . . the prosperity of the last five years in San Francisco has been phenomenal. It is not believed that men of such blood and antecedents are going to subside into inactivity and still less that they will abandon the city they have been so brilliantly and daringly building. . . . The brains, the skill, the cool, hard, poker-playing nerve of it all have been thoroughly awakened. A correspondent observed yesterday, "In any event they show little emotion." That is the strong man's way.

Federal and city forces were not alone in organizing active help for the suffering city. The Southern Pacific Railroad under its president, Harriman, mobilized all its strength to help San Francisco. Not only did it carry relief stores—reaching the city from all over America in immense quantities—free of charge, but the trains that brought in stores carried away people. Anyone in the city whose home was in another state, and who wished to return there, was carried without payment on the railroad, and on the second day after the Disaster seventy passengers were moved every minute in trains totaling ten miles in length. Cars were crammed, and passengers who could not get into them sat on the roof. Harriman, having given his orders, decided to go himself to San Francisco with the utmost speed, and though in those days it was a long journey he arrived on Sunday and was able to see some of the results of his initiative. During the nine days following the earthquake 300,000 free passengers were carried by the Southern Pacific line alone and it was undoubtedly the brilliant handling of the railroads that helped to win the battle of the homeless. The magnitude of the operation can be understood when it is realized that the railroad station in the city itself only took people directly to Los Angeles. The transcontinental railroad ended at Oakland, across the Bay, and, though it was possible in a roundabout sort of way to enter San Francisco directly by railroad from the main continent via Los Angeles, it was much more direct to ferry passengers across the Bay to Oakland. After the earthquake this was no easy matter.

Small personal incidents still lent color to the interminable ordeal. Polly Harts (later Mrs. Robert Earl) lived up on a hill with her family; but, even so, by Friday her parents had decided that the risk to their safety was too great to be taken. So they moved to the Presidio where Captain Harts had a friend who would accommodate them. The Presidio, at the northern end of the city, was already crammed with refugees, and the Harts family felt that they were fortunate to get in. They managed to get transportation from a very reluctant Chinese, and so they were able to take luggage with them. As Mrs. Harts was hourly expecting a baby this was really essential, if they were to move at all, and after a search for Polly (who did not want to leave home and was calmly dressing her doll on the third floor) the whole party piled into a democrat. That night, while the little girl and her brother slept on mattresses on the floor, Mrs. Harts' second son was born. They had moved just in time.

Captain Harts was uneasy about the safety of his house and went back into town every day to see if things were all right and to make sure that their silver had not been looted. And every evening Polly went out to meet her father on his return; if he had a carnation in his buttonhole, picked from the garden at home, the family knew on sight that all was still well. Their luck held, for not only did the newly born baby and his mother flourish in the rough and ready surroundings to which they had fled, but their house in town and all their silver were untouched throughout the conflagration.

At eleven o'clock on Friday night a young journalist, Mary Edith Griswold, instead of remaining in the safety of the camp in which she had taken refuge, set out on an exploring expedition. "The first startling sight," she said, "was a rose garden with hundreds of huge roses glowing red in the light of the flames. We went so close to the fire that I felt my hair curl. We saw some people loot a grocery and bar—the proprietor inviting everyone in to help themselves. There were no lights, only that ghastly light coming in the windows of the fire across the street." Newspaperwoman though she was, her experiences made Miss Griswold feel sick. She saw, for example, many dogs and cats which had been abandoned or forgotten by their owners and which ran back to certain death in the burning buildings when she tried to approach them. Late at night she went back to her camp again. More experiences were in store for her there, for a span of horses broke their tethering straps and came charging into the camp toward her. "We frightened them away with umbrellas which we were using for tents," she explained. And later that night: "It was a most wonderful sight! Many miles—a limitless space of blue flames with the last red glow of big timbers between—of dancing palpitating, living light."

What Miss Griswold did not see, but what might have infinitely amused her, was a little impromptu concert being given by two refugees in the street. One was playing on an old piano rescued from a burning house while the other gave a hearty rendering of "My Merry Oldsmobile," one of the popular songs of the day.

An element of sport was not lacking from the days of the Disaster. When the waterfront buildings were all burning, swarms of rats, full of the wise instinct that never fails them, left in their thousands and made off across town. Ratcatchers were at once set to work, but the job was too big for them and the vast army of hungry rats infested private houses looking for food to replace the piles of garbage they had previously been gorged with in the docks. Orders were at once issued to householders whose homes were far enough from the fire to be a safe refuge for rats (even if their owners did not feel too safe in them) to kill as many as possible each day by every means at their command. Each morning the professional ratcatchers came along and collected the corpses. The thing developed into something of a sporting competition, and Leonora Chase, the child who had been so fascinated by impromptu street kitchens, remembered it well. Her father fancied himself as a shot and every evening after a tiring day's work attending to his medical duties, he would take his shotgun and post himself, his small daughter beside him, at their living-room window. From there he spent a happy hour shooting at the army of rats that invaded his back yard. They were large rats—so large, in fact, that they seemed as big as small cats—and her father had a most appreciative audience for his hour of sport. Mr. Chase might well have been the inspiration for the motto chalked up on many of the food kitchens: *Make the best of it, forget the rest of it.*

Still the conflagration spread and in the mounting tragedy of the dying city smoke constantly turned day into a false twilight. Cinders as large as pennies were falling about the streets. Fourteen miles away in Mill Valley, Ethel McAllister, who had been sent there with her brothers and sisters for safety, frequently played with sheets of printed paper from books, and even pages of music, that had been blown into the air by the five-mile-high fire in the city and only came down to earth again many miles away. The children thought it was marvelous and vied with one another to see who could collect the largest number of "papers from heaven."

By Friday evening the telegraph wires were reopened. There were now twenty-five thousand private messages awaiting delivery from people who had been half mad with anxiety for three whole days. It was a great relief to be in contact with the outside world again, all the more so since things in the city looked as hopeless as ever when Saturday dawned. Fire was still in command, and in spite of the cheerful Californian spirit that had borne all the troubles of those dreadful days, people were despondent. They had all but lost heart; as for the firemen, they were in despair. The fine, dry weather continued, and in spite of their utmost efforts they could accomplish little. Rudi Schubert, back on duty after his short rest in the Presidio, could not see any end to it. It seemed to him that the whole city would be destroyed unless rain came; he wondered sadly when he would see his young wife; normal life appeared so far away that it was almost impossible to think of having a home again in which to be happy.

There was still much to be done in buildings wrecked by the earthquake. Around the Post Office, where Postmaster Fish was laboring to try to restore some sort of order to the mails, there was an immense pile of debris untouched since the early hours of Wednesday. At last the rescuers, who had been working night and day, determined to make a great effort to shift it in case anyone or anything had been buried underneath. It was a hard and heavy job. Little by little the brick and stones were cleared away, and presently the workers thought they saw some slight movement below it all. Could there be anyone alive there? After three full days was it possible that someone who had been buried might have survived?

It was with great excitement that the crowd gathered about the rescue party at work around the Post Office. No one had anything to do during the long, long days and it was a treat to have something to watch. When it became known that the rescuers thought they had detected a movement underneath the heavy pile, the excitement in the crowd grew to fever pitch. And presently, to their amazement and their stupefaction, no less than eight postal clerks were dug out of their three-day grave. They were not only all alive, but in such good shape, considering their terrible ordeal, that prompt and efficient hospital care could soon put them right again.

It was the first gleam of cheer in that dark week and the rescue had a tonic effect on everyone. If men could be rescued alive, and indeed comparatively unharmed, from one building many more might still be found. Casualties might not, after all, be so high as had at first been feared.

So great had been the confusion since the Disaster, and so much concentration had gone into efforts to extinguish the ruinous conflagration, that no official attempt had been made so far to discover the number and identity of the missing. There were many families who had been separated from

177

their relatives since the earthquake hit the city and the uncertainty of the whereabouts of their loved ones, coupled with the deadly anxiety of the fire, made life hard to bear. The Ferry lists were private, not official action. Mayor Schmitz and his Relief Committee had been so busy with other things that they had had no time to make a tally of the citizens—to find out who had left, and who had not been heard of, since the earthquake.

Meanwhile the fire itself showed signs of slackening its fury. Was the ordeal nearly over? Might life still become normal again before long? It now seemed so, and the confident spirit of San Franciscans began to return. But the elements that tortured the city were not yet satisfied. All too soon the trade winds were blowing with all their force. Flames that had been "put out" were revived from the glowing ashes fanned by the strong breeze; in short, the conflagration was undefeated. After the excitement of the day people were plunged into despair all the darker because of the wonderful hope which for a time had cheered the whole city.

The rich men who lived in the comparative safety of Nob Hill were among the only fortunate people in San Francisco. True, they had been alarmed by the earthquake and, like everyone else, dreaded further shocks. But it was easy for them to move out of their mansions into the sun-

light of their fine grounds overlooking the chaos beneath. Many of these men were on the Relief Committee, and worked hard and long to save the city;
but others, those favored ones who possessed yachts,
quickly moved themselves and their families out of
danger onto the blue waters of the Bay.

Much less happy were the owners of the palaces
on Van Ness. That wide avenue was the chosen
place where it was hoped that the fire might be arrested. But this meant that most of the houses on
the south side must be dynamited.

Mrs. Rudolph Spreckels, wife of the sugar king,
found herself in an embarrassing and frightening
situation. Her house on Van Ness was, she knew,
one of the next to be blown up. She was in labor,
and hospitals were so full that they had no room
for a mere confinement—even if Mrs. Spreckels had
liked the idea of entering one. She was fortunate in
having an Irish midwife available to look after
her, and on Saturday afternoon her son was born
—the longed-for heir to the Spreckels fortune. The
Irishwoman never lost her country's characteristic
piety and sense of humor even in the anxious emergency. "God sends earthquakes and babies," she remarked, "but He might in His mercy cut out sending
both of them together."

The eye of a photographer, like that of an artist,
is trained to quick and minute observation. Arnold Genthe, after being forced first from his studio

and then from the St. Francis Hotel by the fire, spent most of his time wandering alone about the city with his camera taking pictures, and watching the reactions of the people in the streets. Their unnatural calm suggested to him that shock following shock had to some extent numbed their sensibilities, and, though the artist in him worked overtime during the fire, it was many weeks before he felt sure that his own mind was functioning normally after the dreadful experience of those four days.

On Saturday night the exhausted fire and rescue teams were roused to make what must have been almost superhuman efforts. The terror had gone on too long; at all costs, at whatever sacrifice, it must be brought to an end. Trade winds might blow, but man's will, fantastically, seemed to conquer the savage determination of the destroying elements. At midnight on Saturday the consistently dry weather of that historic week broke, and it began to rain. If it continued into a steady downpour the fire would be beaten.

But the refugees, huddled together in the camps, were disinclined to be optimistic after their previous disappointment. The rain seemed to condemn them to utter misery, and they sat dumbly in their dripping tents while the broken streets ran with water and chasms left by the earthquake were turned into miniature wells. Sanitary problems at once became far more acute and the Relief Committee itself was sick with worry until, on Sunday morning, it was apparent that at last the tide of fire had turned for good.

Romance bloomed again that day and it was called Wedding Sunday. Couples who had rushed for licenses at the beginning of the Disaster were at last able to use them, and clergy were kept busy all day marrying people in any church that had been left in a usable condition. Most of the newlyweds had no homes to live in. But tents might perhaps be found: in any case, the great thing was to get married.

The sky was at last clear over the Mission District, but a thick pall of smoke still hung over much of the city. Nevertheless people took heart again. The fire was out, the monster was dead, this time for good. In the camps jokes were cracked again with typical Californian humor.

Mayor Schmitz at once issued a proclamation heralding the new hope that dawned that Sunday morning:

To the Citizens of San Francisco:
The fire is now under control and all danger is passed. The only fear is that other fires may start should people build fires in their stoves, and I therefore want all citizens not to build fires in their stoves until the chimneys have been inspected and repaired properly. All citizens are

urged to discountenance the building of fires. I congratulate the citizens of San Francisco upon the fortitude they have displayed and urge upon them the necessity of aiding the authorities in the work of relieving the destitute and suffering.

The proclamation acted like a tonic on the weary city and the old humor began to re-emerge at once. A whisky house which had remained standing, though everything on all four sides of it had burned, put out the following topical rhyme which was highly characteristic of the historic moment:

> If, as some say, God spanked the town
> For being over-frisky
> Why did He burn the churches down
> And save Hotaling's whisky?

People soon left the camps and went out and about again, and many began digging for "treasure"—in most cases their own lost belongings in the ruins. Ben Campbell, a Negro, chose a spot near the railroad track at Townsend Street. After some hard work Ben succeeded in locating what had evidently been a grocery warehouse which, though deeply buried by the earthquake, still had its contents more or less intact. The place was so full of food that joyful onlookers, heedless (now the fire was out) of any penalty they might incur, fell upon the uncovered delicacies. Among other things there were oysters, canned asparagus, beans, and fruit of every description, all "done to a turn" and entirely suitable for a small celebration on the day that San Francisco's long agony was over.

When San Franciscans now began to look around the city they found that all the principal monuments were either completely destroyed, or charred and blackened almost beyond recognition. All newspaper plants were burned out and a combined *Call-Chronicle-Examiner* was being issued from the office of the *Oakland Tribune*. The *Call* skyscraper, though the walls still stood, was completely gutted. The Bohemian Club, with many of its treasures, as well as all the other clubs except the Cosmos and the Century were gone. The Opera House, including the valuable costumes of the ill-fated Metropolitan Opera Company, together with the other theatres which had enlivened life in San Francisco were destroyed. The famous Mechanics Pavilion was a mass of ruins. The Palace, the St. Francis and all the famous hotels were ruined. One old landmark, almost alone, was untouched in the very heart of the devastated area. The columns of the Mission Dolores stood erect upon the apex of its roof: the small slender pillars built long ago by the Spaniards never fell.

Not a single life, it appeared, had been lost in the steel-framed buildings—a fact that encouraged the city to hope that by rebuilding in that modern style no comparable tragedy could ever happen again.

Among famous private residents whose houses were saved was Mrs. Robert Louis Stevenson. She was accustomed to live all the year round in her house on Russian Hill but she happened to be away on that April day when the earthquake rocked and ruined the city. Not having heard of the full extent of the Disaster she made great but (happily for her) unsuccessful attempts to get home again during the week. In the meantime her house was saved for her by a score of members of the Bohemian Club who, knowing she was away, worked desperately to preserve it for her in memory of their beloved R.L.S.

Polly Harts' home was not burned either, possibly because of the constant vigilance of her engineer father. When the family was back home again she returned to school and amused herself by jumping over the great cracks in the streets and sidewalks. Children, on the whole, took the tragedy lightly enough, but when Polly was taken downtown to see the destruction she burst into a torrent of sobbing for a reason she herself was hardly able to understand.

Before the Disaster there had been sinister rumors in the city about what went on in the gaudy streets of Chinatown. It had been said that the police themselves were never able to penetrate cellars which might sometimes be a hundred feet deep and passages where a man might run for as much as an hour without emerging into daylight. Countless opium dens were believed to exist, and after the conflagration dreadful tales were told of men and women burned to death while lying prostrate on couches, lost in day-long, stupefying, yet delicious dreams.

The truth about Chinatown proved to be otherwise. Undoubtedly many yellow people were burned to death in the complete destruction of their narrow quarter, and it is probable that the true number of casualties was never known. The unfortunate crib girls were left to escape as best they could when their rich masters fled for their lives, and not all of them could have got away in time.

But when Chinatown lay in ruins it was, at last, thoroughly explored and mapped out by the responsible authorities—a thing that had never been done before. Not a single underground passage was discovered, and no cellar was found larger than those common in ordinary private houses. The underground dens which had so excited the curiosity of tourists had all been fakes, cleverly planned by the cunning Chinese to stimulate interest and attract custom. The dens were so arranged that a visitor in search of pleasure and excitement was convinced that he was being led along innumerable, dangerous underground passages tenanted by evil-looking Chinese (it was easy for a Chinese to look evil to a Westerner) carrying knives and hatchets and providing a deliciously authentic atmosphere. It was all an illusion, but it had proved completely convincing to the tourists, who were always able to tell horrifying stories of their adventures on their return home.

Chinatown was not the mystery it had been said to be, but it was certainly not a pretty place, and San Francisco was all the better without it. But the extraordinary and almost unbelievable fact was that, even after the whole area was cleared away after the Disaster, prostitution and slavery continued more or less openly among the Chinese in the city right up to the time that the Red Light Abatement Act was passed by the California legislature in 1914. Then, and only then, an effective legal weapon existed, and at last there could be no more slave girls. Nevertheless, although there were always many Chinese and their women in a city that looked toward the Orient, the Disaster destroyed the old Chinatown forever. Steel-framed buildings, new skyscrapers and modern luxury houses sprang up in a remarkably short time, and the fabled place of underground passages was never rebuilt or included in any plans for the new San Francisco.

The citizens, weary in body and exhausted in spirit, who climbed up the slopes of Nob Hill on that Sunday morning, April 23rd, to survey what was left of their city saw a grimly forbidding scene spread before them. Instead of a mass of buildings, with streets cleft this way and that between them, there was now an almost total desolation to south and west. The texture of a city, varied a thousand times by roofs and chimneys, had given place to a gray, flat area of almost total devastation. Here and there some object stood up to point a frightful contrast—a gutted skyscraper; an isolated house not wholly burned out; even a tree, blackened by heat and smoke. But apart from these few accents, and they were very few, what had been San Francisco was now an empty plain crisscrossed by streets which, after being torn by the earthquake and piled high with debris, came from nowhere, led nowhere, and intersected each other aimlessly. Everywhere the haze of smoke still hovered thick; everywhere the smell of charred timber hung strongly in the air which the rain had freshened. In five days old San Francisco had disappeared.

NINE

ON the Sunday after the Disaster the fire was out and the streets were damp and miserable with rain. Five days of fear, danger and apprehension had left thousands tired and apathetic. Only young lovers were fully animated; they had survived to be married and for them at least life was good.

For countless others Sunday was a day of grim stocktaking. They had lost their homes, their clothes and their furniture. It was hard, as they looked about the ravaged city where the ground was still hot and smoke still rose, to wager anything on the future—even for San Franciscans who so dearly loved to gamble. Hardly a man could tell how much he was really worth. There were too many imponderables to be resolved before anything like a true estimate could be made.

Actual money was extremely short. No one had any available cash, and even if a man was lucky enough to possess a twenty-dollar bill it was almost impossible to get it changed. There had been such a run on the banks by citizens wanting to get their money out on the first day of the Disaster that all banks were at once closed, and San Franciscans beat in vain against the closed doors that held their fortunes. The Government declared a public holiday and went on extending it from day to day until some sort of order could be put into the financial chaos. The banks themselves were mostly in poor shape after the conflagration. Out of five hundred and seventy-six vaults and safes opened in the district east of Powell and north of Market Street, 40 per cent were said to have given ineffective protection against the great fire and were found to contain nothing but heaps of ashes. Some buildings had been completely destroyed, and the vaults of others were red-hot and impossible of access for days.

The mood of the citizens was changing. They had been extraordinarily patient and almost unnaturally well-disciplined during their time of trial. They had been full of gratitude to the authorities for the stern and just measures which had assured order and provided something for all to eat in their extremity. But now that the Disaster was over, shocked minds began to revive. Patience— which had seemed the only way to bear what had to be borne—gave place to a new and healthy spirit of dissatisfaction with the sort of existence that had been forced upon them. There was a strong wish to start at once to rebuild not only houses but also a more tolerable way of living.

Enormously exaggerated stories had circulated about the number of casualties during San Francisco's week of agony, and for some time it was beyond anyone's power to contradict them with authority. Indeed the accurate total never could be given, for many had been burned in wrecked houses and many bodies were buried without permission and never reported. It was widely known that at least three hundred bodies had been taken from the bad district south of Market Street, but for the rest, it soon became happily evident that far fewer people had lost their lives in San Francisco than could have been believed possible in view of the magnitude of the catastrophe that had struck the city. Much later, when all records had been carefully checked, it was announced that considerably more than five hundred, though certainly less than a thousand, persons had lost their lives, and that was as near an estimate as could ever be given.

Material damage, however, was enormous. A total area of over four square miles had been burned out and about 28,188 houses destroyed. Even after the fire was declared out, the authorities were so nervous lest it should revive again that each standing house in the city had to have an official certificate of safety (a copy of which was preserved by the California Historical Society) for its chimneys before a fire could be lighted indoors. The inspection for a certificate took a considerable time and added not a little to the impatience of those citizens lucky enough still to have their homes.

According to later estimates the earthquake had destroyed $20,000,000 worth of property, while earthquake and fire together accounted for no less than $400,000,000 of loss. Small wonder that in the time of their first great trial, such insurance offices as still stood were besieged and, once the fire had subsided, insurance men were among the most worried people in San Francisco. It was up to them, as they well knew, to pay as much and as quickly as possible. With their companies distributed all over the world and communications with that world still difficult, this was no easy question for the men on the spot to settle. To their everlasting credit, claims were promptly and fully met wherever it was humanly possible; and to everyone's immense

191

relief, insurance, then still a comparative novelty, worked. The reputations of companies that paid at once soared, while those few who did not honor their obligations found that their business had disappeared.

In spite of banking difficulties the situation was not too desperate, and in addition to the money existing in San Francisco itself funds from outside soon began to flow into the city at an astonishing rate. A total sum of about $185,244,198 was received, there being 5,411 corporate and individual subscriptions. The Government's contribution, at first fixed at $1,000,000, was quickly raised to $2,500,000 owing to President Roosevelt's personal intervention. Roosevelt also wisely abandoned his first plan of allowing a single agency—the Red Cross—to control financial aid to the city. It was soon apparent that such a deluge of money was coming in that no single society could possibly hope to handle the situation with the necessary promptness and efficiency. "The need of employing the Red Cross, save as an auxiliary," proclaimed the President, "has passed, and I urge that hereafter all contributions from any source be sent direct to James D. Phelan, chairman Finance Committee, San Francisco. Mr. Devine, of the Red Cross, will disburse any contributions sent to him through former Mayor Phelan and will work in accord with him in all ways."

The President's proclamation was greatly appreciated in the stricken city, for it was an official tribute to the committee of citizens who had worked so well and so tirelessly throughout the Disaster. It also restored confidence in the city's ability to look after itself financially, and thereafter everything went much more smoothly. Later on, in June, the Government placed as much as $22,000,000 at the disposal of San Francisco for reconstruction; it was quickly realized that the city was one of America's great assets and that the sooner it could be put to rights again the better it would be for all.

In addition to the Government's contributions and those of many of the cities and private citizens of America, there were, possibly for the first time, sums of relief money from many labor organizations. To take two examples at random: the United Brotherhood of Carpenters and Joiners of Indianapolis gave $10,000, while the United Mineworkers also sent a substantial contribution to help the mining city that had suffered such terrible loss.

Gradually the banks were reopened and the money situation improved, after one or two initial muddles and mistakes—the result, no doubt, of tired brains and bodies. For example, $40,000 of relief money was spent on whisky in the first hectic days, and afterward no one could remember who ordered it or for what purpose. Since alcohol could obviously not be distributed free except in the most urgent medical cases, the whisky was eventually sold at auction and the profits (which were probably considerable, since everyone wanted a drink) given to hospitals.

By Sunday physical conditions in the city had improved and it was hardly possible to believe that only two days earlier the *Oakland Examiner* had proclaimed not only that there was an epidemic of scarlet fever in the city, but that the putrefying bodies of horses and cattle killed by earthquake and fire were causing horrible stenches, that many bodies remained unburied about the streets, and that the dearth of fresh water was causing much sickness. Not only were there no epidemics of any kind—mainly because of the prompt and stern measures of health authorities—but all bodies, whether human or animal, had been buried, and the Crystal Springs water reservoir, broken by the movement of the fault, had been repaired, so that drinking water was available for all, though still in relatively short supply and with little to spare for washing.

Long lines of tables were established in most open spaces and food relief stations were busy— for there was no food except what was officially distributed. It was not scarce, but the authorities saw that they might have to care for homeless thousands for an indefinite period and they determined to take no chances of supplies running out.

194

An old Frenchman went to one of the relief stations, wanting to buy a five-cent loaf of bread.

"How many in your family?" the man was asked.

"Seex—please sell me the bread."

"Dozen and a half eggs, five bread, pound butter, three pounds bacon, four beans, two rice, two sugar *and* a half coffee," droned out the relief boss.

"What is that? I am no beggar! Here is the money."

"Say, old man, you're broke, maybe we're all broke, but this is Uncle Sam, *he* ain't broke!"

The old Frenchman was touched and nearly overcome with gratitude, for he and his family had been hungry and he could hardly believe his good fortune. He bared his head. "I take off my hat to Uncle Sam," he said as he went off with his provisions.

Though food was not at once being sold in shops, the same rule did not apply to clothing. Leonora Chase, the child who had so much enjoyed cooking in the street, was taken by her mother down to Van Ness Avenue where so many of the grand old palaces had been blown up to try to stop the fire, but a few remained. These were very large and were at once turned into makeshift shops to help out citizens who had to have clothing. You could be fitted with a new suit in a bathroom and Leonora, to her immense delight, had a new pair of shoes bought for her in a vast room with, as she well remembered, a beautiful crystal chandelier hanging in it which oddly enough had survived the effect of the earthquake. Leonora, who had never seen such a thing before, did not realize it, but chandeliers were generally considered among the most perishable of belongings in an earthquake, yet she always remembered one that was saved.

Corpses had been buried, but many streets of blackened, sooty buildings were still full of mounds of debris. It was all too plain that nothing approaching normal life could be resumed in San Francisco until a beginning had been made to clear the place up. The Committee prepared to do its official part, but one energetic citizen had an idea of his own and performed the probably unparalleled feat of carrying it out. Market Street, one of the most important streets in the city, was also one of the worst hit by the Disaster. Almost all the buildings were desolate, broken, and unfit for use, but there was no reason why traffic should not circulate. That, at least, would make things seem more normal, but first the piles of debris had to be cleared. In order to do this every able-bodied citizen who passed that way was unofficially asked to work for a level twenty minutes with shovel and cart in order to do his bit to help. Evidently the men of San Francisco approved of that particular bit of private enterprise, for within half a day Market Street was cleared for traffic.

By April 26th the San Francisco *Chronicle* was triumphantly reporting official progress in clearing the city and getting life back to something approaching what it had been before. The headlines speak for themselves:

STREETCARS TO RUN TODAY
ELECTRIC LIGHTING TO BE RESUMED
IN THREE DISTRICTS TONIGHT
FORTY TELEPHONES IN OPERATION
YESTERDAY

That issue cheered people up a great deal, and on April 29th the *Call* had more news of the gigantic efforts being made to restore and clear the city. The Mile Rock, it announced, had been chosen as the main dumping ground for debris, and great barges had been commandeered to carry out the work. The first load had left several days earlier, towed by the gallant tug *Sea Fox,* with 2,000 tons of debris, and more barges were to go into commission. Until the rubbish was cleared it was useless to think about rebuilding, and everyone determined that not a moment should be lost.

For even in those first difficult days no one ever doubted that San Francisco would be rebuilt and become even better and more famous than she had been before. As Lawrence W. Harris told the California Historical Society in 1956, "San Fran-

cisco shook off the earthquake as a dog with a
bone, and then buried all thought of it." And Mr.
Harris spoke from his own experience, for he had
been there and was the author of a cheerful little
poem that went the rounds of the city on a printed
card which many San Franciscans still cherish:

Put me somewhere west of East Street where there's noth-
    ing left but dust,
Where the lads are all a hustlin' and where everything's
    gone bust,
Where the buildin's that are standin' sort of blink and
    blindly stare
At the damndest finest ruins ever gazed on anywhere.

Bully ruins—brick and wall—through the night I've
    heard you call
Sort of sorry for each other 'cause you had to burn and
    fall,
From the Ferries to Van Ness you're a Godforsaken mess,
But the damndest finest ruins—nothin' more or nothin'
    less.

The strangers who come rubberin' and a huntin' souvenirs,
The fools they try to tell us it will take a million years
Before we can get started, so why don't we come to live
And build our homes and factories upon land they've got
    to give.

"Got to give"! Why on my soul, I would rather bore a hole
And live right in the ashes than even move to Oakland's
    mole,
If they'd all give me the pick of their buildin's proud
    and slick
In the damndest finest ruins still I'd rather be a brick!

It was not the finest poetry but it exactly, expressed the mood of San Franciscans in April 1906. Mr. Harris's poem showed a certain jaunty pride and a refusal to be beaten which was characteristic of the feelings of his fellow citizens. Today when the old-timers show the card to a stranger they have a faraway light in their eyes as they remember that heroic time.

Another famous San Franciscan (though not a native of the city), the handsome Arnold Genthe, felt much the same way as Lawrence Harris. He had been out and about in San Francisco during the whole Disaster, roaming the streets with his camera and catching the mood of the desperate days with the unfailing skill of an artist. And when the fire was out and he at length returned to his old studio, only to find it burned out, it never occurred to him to leave the city that he had grown to love. He simply looked about for somewhere else to live in what remained of San Francisco until finally he found a cottage near the Presidio and settled down there to watch and help in the work of reconstruction.

The citizens were justifiably proud of themselves and determined to rebuild San Francisco as soon as possible. They had patiently endured a disaster which at the beginning of the century seemed unequaled in horror. And it had been hard to endure, for man likes to be able to fight back when he is attacked and his whole life menaced. It was impossible to fight the earthquake, and when the dreaded fire took over, the puny means at the disposal of the city made it impossible to fight that either. Like the citizens of London in their shelters while bombs rained down upon them, San Franciscans could only watch and pray. Fortunately, America was proud of them and fully conscious of their predicament. No other site nor any other city could be so important to the continent as a rebuilt, improved San Francisco, and the men at the top were quick to realize it and provide a generous amount of help.

Long before the Disaster the natural advantages of the city with its matchless harbor were known to the world. Its pre-eminence, largely owing to the fact that the depth of the water on the San Francisco side was so much greater than that on the farther side of the Bay, was undisputed. The necessities of trade and commerce, especially with China and the Orient, would have compelled the rebuilding of the city even had its citizens been less enthusiastic about the project. But enthusiastic they were, and not least the big businessmen who had suffered such huge losses through the Disaster that their insurance would go hardly any way at all toward covering them.

Mayor Schmitz put out one more proclamation to the world. He was nearly at the end of his brief period of honor and glory, after which he was to sink again into the climate of suspicion and distrust from which he never emerged. But the Disaster was his finest hour and he was one of its heroes. San Francisco will be rebuilt, he announced. A new and greater city will speedily rise to take the place of the old. That was his message, and he was right; in no time at all his prophecy was on its way to realization.

"All talk of abandoning the city for some such place as Seattle is foolish," said Archer M. Huntington, whose house containing many valuable treasures had been destroyed. "San Francisco is the logical metropolis west of the Rockies. The city will be rebuilt at once and it will be an improved city."

His words were echoed by a chorus of such well-known names as Crocker, Spreckels, Ogden Mills, and Guggenheim—to mention only a few of them. It was evident that the city had powerful friends and supporters. It would rise like the Phoenix from its ashes and, as a brave gesture of confidence, the magical bird itself was adopted as the official seal of the city.

The place would be rebuilt, but how should it be done? Many of the old ideas, the frame houses, the redwood timbers, and the brick veneers, had proved themselves untrustworthy. Although many frame houses were put up again, something altogether new must be employed for the business section.

Although the San Andreas fault had not at that time been so accurately mapped or so closely studied as has since been done, the authorities now knew for certain that San Francisco was earthquake country and that in consequence special care would be necessary in building it up again. The coastal ranges west of the Rockies were the newest part of the American continent—"new" being employed in the widest geological sense. Mountains were still being formed and the territory was not yet completely established in what might be its ultimate form. The fault, indeed both the faults, for the Hayward as well as the San Andreas had to be taken into account, were a constant danger, and though the business district of San Francisco was about eight miles away from the nearest of them it had been almost entirely destroyed by the earthquake. This was an ominous fact which clearly demonstrated the care that must be taken in rebuilding the city in the strongest possible way in relation to the danger from any future tremors that might occur.

The danger of made or filled land had also been demonstrated in the Disaster. The extreme narrowness of the city site made it difficult to see how such land could be dispensed with. Increased trade must inevitably bring increased population and

202

more business houses, and more room would have to be found for them somewhere. But it was hoped that key buildings, at least, would not be built upon filled and therefore particularly vulnerable land.

Some two years before the earthquake there had been a concerted movement among the citizens of San Francisco to beautify the city that had largely grown up haphazard during the gold rush. They formed the Association for the Improvement and Adornment of San Francisco, and they invited Daniel Hudson Burnham, a famous "builder of cities," to give his ideas on their particular problem. A bungalow was built for him and his assistants on Twin Peaks, several hundred feet above the level of the streets, from which they could command a splendid view of the city and form some idea of its possibilities. Not unnaturally, Mr. Burnham developed a great love for San Francisco in the months during which he watched the city in sunlight and cloud from his eyrie on Twin Peaks, and he made no secret of the fact that he considered it one of the finest natural sites in the world. No words, he was reported to have said, could do justice to its marvelous natural beauty and the possibilities which it offered.

Apparently the vertical lines on which the city had developed offended the beauty-loving citizens of San Francisco and they wanted something altogether more European. In fact, what they really wanted was a sort of Paris of the West, with broad boulevards, great parkways and wooded heights —a city of sunken gardens, of airy bridges, of stately gardens and broad expanses. Mr. Burnham, who, it should quickly be added, was not all lyrical fancy but also a most practical man with a good eye for the civic and business requirements of such a city as San Francisco, had just submitted his plan for beautifying the place when it was overtaken by the Disaster. It was immediately evident that what had been planned to take many years would have to be done as fast as possible. In the event, San Francisco developed along vertical lines as before, and with singularly few trees of any size, but at least it was a planned reconstruction that was carried out.

As to the type of building to be erected on the four-mile site which had been devastated by fire, it was only necessary to look around the ruins to see which had suffered least in the Disaster. The tall, steel-framed buildings that had been erected at the end of the nineteenth century were still standing, though they had been gutted by fire and it was not at once certain how much they were out of the true. The steel-framed *Call* building stood up well, and the *Chronicle* building, though not steel-framed, was so strengthened at each floor level that it had enough stability to withstand the earthquake shock.

Engineers and contractors lost no time in sending representatives to San Francisco so that the authorities might have the very best, most modern advice. Expense in those days was hardly thought of, and the work was swift indeed in comparison to the rebuilding of modern towns after the devastation of recent years. But it was fully understood that rebuilding alone would not be enough. The most important thing was to make every effort to safeguard the water supply in case such an emergency ever arose in the future.

The damage done by the earthquake—a disaster against which there could be no insurance—was as nothing compared with what the fire had accomplished. The combination of the two elements was indeed formidable, and earth and fire must never be allowed the opportunity of working together again. Fires had happened time and time again in the history of the city, but such a conflagration as that of 1906 was a thing which man, however feeble he might be before the forces of nature, might surely be able to prevent.

TEN

"PAPA! PAPA!" cried the wife and daughter of a sober-minded citizen during the Disaster. "It's the end of the world. We are going to die!"

Papa smiled at them gently. "Well, what of it? Aren't we going to die in San Francisco?"

That little story fairly represents the feelings of those who have spent their lives in the great city of the West. And if anyone in America were to speak of "the good old days," as is so frequently done in Europe, it might well be the old-timers of San Francisco. The early days of the city have taken on the

206

quality of wonder: they bring back memories of an enchanted life in a rich enchanted city. Old Chinatown, the Barbary Coast and the gambling dens have acquired a patina of strange excitement, and those who talk about the time before 1906 have a certain lilt in their voice and a light in their eyes that is unmistakable. Even the terrible days of the earthquake and fire, at this remove, are chiefly memorable as having been a unique experience, sharply etched but with much of the strain and horror taken out of them.

Today San Francisco is prosperous—though the docks are not so full as they might be owing to the loss of the China trade, and the gold fields are worked out. It is no longer devil-may-care and "frisky," to use the old expression, but it is gay and lively. Theatres, the opera, clubs and libraries flourish and are an integral part of life in the city which is so far away from New York that the influence of the metropolis, its extraordinary, irresistible attraction, is hardly felt. For a European the cultural and social life of San Francisco, combined with its natural beauty, must have a unique appeal.

Along the checkered course of the twentieth century there have been many earth tremors in California, and San Francisco has had its fair share of them, as is always bound to be the case owing to its proximity to the San Andreas fault. But until

the morning of Friday, March 22, 1957, a beautiful
sunny day when everyone went to work as usual
and cars poured over the bridges without the slightest fear, nothing at all serious had been recorded.
On that day the city was rocked by the worst shock
since the Disaster of 1906 when the whole place
had nearly perished. True, the shock was very much
less than that of the one fifty-one years earlier;
and its magnitude was only 5.5 against 8.25 of the
great earthquake. But it was quite enough to strike
fear into a good many hearts in San Francisco.
And it might have caused many more casualties,
for instead of occurring in the early hours of the
morning when most people were still in bed and the
streets empty, danger struck at 11:45—at the peak
hour of the day when business people were hard at
work in the offices, shoppers were out and about
everywhere, and housewives were, perhaps, taking
a moment of leisure after completing their early
chores.

As always, there was no warning, and the city
was entirely unprepared for the shock which might
well have spelled its doom. But nearly everyone
knew at once what was happening, and reacted
according to their natures. Miss Trimble, Staff As-
sistant at the California Historical Society on Jack-
son Street, knew a good deal about earthquakes.
She had been in the violent tremor that had occurred at Long Beach in the south and, having

survived that unharmed, she judged that she knew exactly what to do and that she need not be unduly frightened. She was sitting at her desk in the beautiful hall of the Society's headquarters when the noise—so well remembered—and the subsequent trembling began, and she at once took a hasty look around to choose her best position. In a flash she saw it: under the magnificently solid staircase was the place for her. So, in a space of time far shorter than it takes to tell, she sat herself down there and only then noticed that she was opposite a very solid-looking statue which was gently but steadily rocking to and fro. The statue never fell, but Miss Trimble watched it in fascinated anxiety for the duration of the shock.

People in cars—so infinitely more numerous than in 1906 when it had been remarked that surprisingly the new monsters did more to save people than to injure them—apparently felt nothing. Mr. Donald McLaughlin, who had watched the Disaster from his home in Berkeley, was driving to San Francisco airport with his secretary that morning on the start of a business trip. He was working as they drove, and neither he nor his secretary felt a thing. On arrival at the airport he was much surprised to be called by his wife (he still lived in Berkeley) and to be asked tenderly if he was safe and the car undamaged. Mrs. McLaughlin realized that in San Francisco the shock must have been of some severity and she was worried about her husband because the airport was built on filled ground and particularly vulnerable to earthquakes.

The enormous building program that had been carried out in the Bay suburbs greatly increased the danger if only because of the enormous population they housed. In addition, the splendid bridges linking the city with its satellites and constantly carrying vast numbers of cars and trucks to and from the city were as yet unproved in an emergency. The beautiful Golden Gate Bridge has one pier built on filled ground and, being a suspension bridge, it is capable of considerable movement caused by the normal traffic that it carries. (There are instruments on the bridge to register normal traffic vibration—and by implication anything more violent.)

On the morning of March 22nd a single man was engaged in painting the very top of the bridge, a fairly nerve-racking assignment at the best of times. At the moment of shock the whole wonderful structure swayed wildly to and fro and the painter's one thought was to get down as fast as possible from his dizzy eminence. But the movement was so great that the climb down was impossible. He just had to hang on desperately until the shock was over and normal conditions restored.

Elizabeth Gaman, a young Englishwoman, lived

in Mill Valley, a lovely Mediterranean-like sub-
urb about ten miles north of the city. Mill Valley
is in Marin County not far from the San Andreas
fault, and the 1957 earthquake gave Elizabeth
the surprise of her life. She had never before been
in any tremor, however small, and the earth to
her was a solid dependable element. She had,
of course, often heard people talk about earthquakes but, like almost everyone else who has
never experienced one, she had given them little
thought and had no idea what the feeling of one
would be like. On the morning of March 22nd Elizabeth was at home (her husband was in the city)
having a cup of coffee with a friend while their two
young children played happily together in a small
adjoining room. Suddenly she was aware of a deep
noise which at first she took to be the sound of
blasting—a thing with which she was perfectly
familiar—but the blasting noise was followed immediately by a most extraordinary shaking. The
coffee in her cup began to waltz up and down until
it finally spilled, she found that she could not keep
her feet firmly on the floor and, as she later wrote
home to her mother in England, she felt just as
though her little house were about to gallop down
the hill into San Francisco. Elizabeth was an experienced young woman who had traveled the
world and seen and felt all manner of things, but
she readily confessed that the earthquake in

March 1957 really frightened her. "Write about an earthquake if you like," she told a friend, "but do try never to be in one."

At the same moment Leonora Chase Wright, the woman who had such vivid memories of the Disaster, was teaching school. As she sat calmly at her desk she felt the floor vibrating and heard what was to her a familiar rumble. Her immediate thought was for the class of young children under her care. At all costs they should not be alarmed. So with a cheerful authoritative word she immediately got them all up onto their feet and merrily started them doing dancing steps, "for a change." They slid and jumped and tried out pirouettes and not one noticed the earthquake. They were doing unusual movements anyway, and the temporary jumping of the floor beneath their feet was translated into their own excited and inexpert movements. Mrs. Wright kept her class at the drill for quite a little while after the shaking ceased, and until they went home and heard it talked about by their elders the children did not realize that there had been an earthquake at all.

Ever since the Disaster the world's eyes had from time to time rested in a sort of fearful fascination upon San Francisco just in case such a terror ever happened again. After the March affair—small though it was—the French magazine *Realités* that covers the world gave its readers a colorful, if exaggerated account, headed *Panic at San Francisco.*

During five hours the whole city was shaken like a drunken vessel. The most violent earthquake registered at San Francisco since 1906 terrified the population. Lampposts oscillated, the arches of the Golden Gate Bridge shook, the clocks all began to strike, the gas mains were broken, fires broke out in many places, schoolchildren scattered, magistrates adjourned their sessions, and the central telephone exchanges were inundated with calls of people mad with fear.

The striking little paragraph was accompanied by a dramatic photograph of a food store in San Francisco where the entire floor space was covered with cans that had been shaken down from their shelves.

Similar stories, suitably modified, were recorded in the press of the world. But the reality was not half so grim.

MORE SAN FRANCISCO QUAKES . . . MAYOR'S EMERGENCY were the *Call's* principal headlines on the day after the first shock. And not altogether without reason, since there had been no less than fifty-two tremors since the preceding day and Mayor Christopher, in common with many other citizens, felt that he should be prepared for the worst. In the tradition of his predecessor Mayor Schmitz, he called an emergency meeting, but happily no great trial awaited the assembled gentlemen. Science, even in the present enlightened days, cannot predict when an earthquake is likely to happen; and since many were quite evidently happening at that moment the Mayor mobilized the Fire Force and the Civil Defense Organization and stayed all day in his office. The police reported that "fear-inspired quiet" seemed to pervade the city, but the switchboards were so jammed with calls that the dial system completely broke down. There was no way of giving priority to official calls; the Police and Fire departments were unable to get into touch with one another, and therefore it was afterward decided to install hand-operated lines to connect the two until the whole telephone system could be properly studied and overhauled. But for private residents unaware of the public difficulty, there was a good deal of anxiety. Marion Schindler, a young married woman who lived in Mill Valley, was at work in the city on the morning of the 1957 earthquake. She had left her young son, Peter, at home, as he was not well, and though a neighbor had promised to run in and see him she tried to call him up in order to make sure of his safety. But not until 4:30 in the afternoon could she get a free line on the telephone.

Citizens got their most reliable news of the situation from the radio. It was too expensive for the city to interrupt and take over the television program,

214

but radio gave out bulletins from which it was soon learned that no serious damage had been done.

In Golden Gate Park stands a relic of the great Disaster, and in 1957 it had an adventure all its own. The "Portals of the Past," as it has come to be called, is in reality the only survival from a private residence on California Street that was entirely destroyed by the fire. The "portal" is a graceful structure of four pairs of pillars crowned by Ionic columns, and it was re-erected in Golden Gate Park as a memento of the past. It stood firm in 1906 but in 1957 one column was knocked down and destroyed by the earthquake.

Little damage of importance was done; the city was neither broken nor in bandages. But many pipe lines in poor or shifting soil—San Francisco's special risk—were broken, and a good deal of plaster and chimney damage was reported. The San Andreas and Hayward faults were once more at the root of the trouble, and the former moved and crept, though no surface faulting was reported to cause renewed anxiety.

"Damage depends on how far you are from an earthquake, how well built your house is and what kind of soil your house is on." San Franciscans thoroughly understand those words, and by 1957 they had taken precautions to see that city buildings were constructed as well as possible to withstand a danger from which they can never be free.

Only in one respect were the two shocks strictly comparable; the clock on the Ferry Building stopped at the moment of the earthquake both at the beginning and the middle of the century.

Many San Franciscans of the Disaster were still there on that March day in 1957. Mrs. Ethel McAllister Grubb enjoyed life in her beautiful old house. Mrs. Leonora Chase Wright was teaching school. Mrs. Snyder delighted in the success of her doctor daughter. Donald McLaughlin still lived in Berkeley and Paul Edwards, the young man from Stanford, lived happily at Los Altos. Mr. Guy Giffen, who was so successful as a midwife in 1906, went in and out of the Pioneer Club, sometimes grumbling, but happy to be in San Francisco, where the climate never forced him to wear a Dacron suit as he would have to in New York.

Rudolph Schubert, ex-Battalion Chief of the San Francisco Fire Department, together with his wife, tended the garden of their charming house. If on that day of the smaller shock in March 1957 his thoughts turned to the water supply, he must have been reassured that so little damage was done.

All questions of business and trade apart, the secret of San Francisco is that people who go there develop a deep love of the city and would rather live there than anywhere else in the world.

INDEX

Index